Industrial Relations in a British Car Factory

by *GARFIELD CLACK*

Research Officer, Department of Applied Economics, Cambridge

CAMBRIDGE
AT THE UNIVERSITY PRESS
1967

PUBLISHED BY

THE SYNDICS OF THE CAMBRIDGE UNIVERSITY PRESS

Bentley House, 200 Euston Road, London N.W. 1

American Branch: 32 East 57th Street, New York, N.Y. 10022

PRODUCED BY Uneoprint
set on electric keyboards
photo-reproduced and printed offset
at The Gresham Press
UNWIN BROTHERS LIMITED
Old Woking   Surrey   England

Contents

PART I

A   Introduction

This paper is a combined product of research into 'the causes of small strikes' and of an interest in the motor industry. Financial support for the research came from what was then the Department of Scientific and Industrial Research. Interest in the car firms arose not only from the rich source of field material which they offered and from the concern being expressed about industrial relations in the motor industry, but also from suggestions in previously published work by H. A. Turner and John Bescoby.(1) Professor Turner gave overall direction to the research, and a book(2) about industrial relations in the car firms has been published. This paper is thus less a report of ongoing research than a case study which is complementary to the book—having contributed to the latter while at the same time drawing on the comments and experience of its co-authors.

It is appropriate here also to thank men and management in the firm to which the study relates for their willingness to be observed and questioned during the research. The comments on earlier drafts of this paper by individuals in the firm, as well as the assistance and comments obtained from various trade union officials and the local employers' association, are greatly appreciated. None of these persons may be mentioned by name, as the firm has requested that it be allowed to remain anonymous in publications of the research findings. Despite all this help, errors of fact and matters of interpretation in this paper remain the responsibility of the author: there are few persons who could be expected to entirely agree with the way in which the material has been selected and handled.

The terms of reference of the research suggested 'participant observation' as a field method to be considered. The author was to take hourly-

_____

(1)   Papers in The Manchester School, May 1961, and Bulletin of the Oxford University Institute of Statistics, May 1961.

(2)   Labour Relations in the Motor Industry: a Study of Industrial Unrest and an International Comparison, H. A. Turner, Garfield Clack, Geoffrey Roberts, (Allen and Unwin, 1967).

paid jobs in factories and examine strikes at first hand. There are obvious advantages of acquiring information in this direct way, but the method is not without its difficulties. For example, who in the field are going to be approached first about the research, and at what stage of the proceedings? The repercussions of these approaches on the field situations have to be borne in mind. The method may also be very time-consuming, while the range of inquiry open to an observer on the workshop floor may be quite limited in the sense that 'external' information highly pertinent to an understanding of events is not readily accessible. Diminishing returns may set in rather sharply for the observer. Then again, there are the hazards of 'going native'—of the observer becoming emotionally committed to particular causes within the situation, commitments which may then impair his research functions.

After a 'pilot run' of manual employment (lasting for several weeks) in an engineering factory, consent was obtained from the shop stewards' conveners and the personnel management to undertake the research in this car-assembly factory. Both parties were fully informed from the start of the nature and purpose of the project; and it was at the conveners' suggestion—endorsed by the personnel management—that, if possible, knowledge about the research and the author's status be narrowly confined for at least an initial (unspecified) period. In the event, the research was explained to departmental management and fellow workers by the author after five weeks at the factory, by which time his social relations on the shop floor had become fairly settled (having extended, for example, to membership of a meal-break soccer group). The knowledge was received with surprisingly casual interest, although the shop management were more cautious in their reactions. There was no apparent resentment or hostility from either management or workers during the whole period of employment at the factory.

The field-work was conducted over a continuous period of seven months, nearly five of which were spent as an hourly-paid worker. Two jobs were held; the first as a storeman in the spare parts department (which occupied a section of the main assembly building), and the second as a storeman in another department which was responsible for supplying stocks of parts and components to a section of one of the main assembly lines. The job in the spare parts stores was acceptable as the first suitable vacancy, and was held for ten weeks because the situation in the department proved to be fruitful for the purpose of the study. The second job permitted a good deal of movement about the factory, and in particular it gave almost unrestricted access to a section of the assembly workers. In both cases the jobs were standard or normal for that type of work, the wages being those in force for storemen. Normal disciplinary sanctions were applied, the only privilege being—after the first five weeks—permission to attend general meetings of shop stewards during working hours.

The final ten weeks at the factory were spent in an attempt to overcome some of the limitations on data gathering which working on the shop floor had imposed. Time was spent with individual shop stewards' conveners engaged on their main business of attending to the interests and grievances of their members, and as a 'silent member' of the factory's Conveners' Committee (which will be described later). Some weeks were spent also as an observer in the Personnel Department. It was possible during most of this final period at the factory to attend joint meetings of shop stewards and management at various levels within the factory, and, on one occasion, between senior management, full-time trade union officials, and shop stewards held at the offices of the local employers' association. Most of the interviewing of individual workers and managers was also undertaken during the final weeks of field-work, although visits were paid to the area and the factory for this purpose after the main field-work had been completed.

A study of strikes—particularly in situations where these occur with any frequency—becomes in effect an examination of the day-to-day conduct of workplace industrial relations. And the strikes may be convenient focal points about which to structure such a wider study. There is, however, a problem of approach. Strikes are complicated social events, and attempts to understand or explain them risk charges of dilletantism on the one hand and myopia on the other. No academic discipline would lay claim to a monopoly of explanatory success, and this is one justification for the phenomenological and eclectic approach of this study. The research resources did not permit—nor did the nature of the project suggest—the use of rigorous questionnaire or statistical techniques. These latter were used in the wider study of the industry's labour relations over forty years, of which this 'participant' research formed only a part. Concentration on a 'social system' or small group approach seemed inappropriate to situations where 'external' influences seemed so important. But the study is unbalanced in the sense that there was little opportunity to examine the processes of managerial decision-making: the research method predisposed a no-longer-fashionable emphasis on workers' rather than on managerial behaviour.

Some further limitations of the study must be acknowledged. Although the author took jobs in other engineering factories, attempts to carry out the research in a similar way in other car firms were frustrated despite lengthy preliminary negotiations. The employment position was sometimes unhelpful; several parties had to agree to the method; the industry was attracting public attention and was increasingly sensitive about outside enquiries. But while it was not possible to work in two car firms for comparative purposes, it was apparent from factory visits that there are no major differences between the plant layout and production techniques of the larger British car-assembly factories—of which the subject of this study is one. For this reason it is possible both to provide—in the next section of the paper—a description of the factory and working environment without danger of identifying the firm, and to suggest that the important differences in industrial relations behaviour between the car firms have to be accounted for in other than technological terms.

Then again, the timing of the study may have been unfortunate. In retrospect, some of the firm's managers and shop stewards have suggested that the period was unrepresentative of conditions at the factory either before or after the field-work was undertaken. It was held that the firm had been expanding its capacity, was re-organising the factory's production facilities, was laying down further assembly lines and putting a new model into production. It was adopting a new paint process, and had made personnel changes in two departments intimately concerned with industrial relations, i.e. the Work Study and Personnel Departments. On the face of it, these seem to be powerful arguments limiting the usefulness of the study. Certainly there were some perceptible strains within the Work Study and Personnel Departments, and between these departments and the shop stewards, which could plausibly be attributed to the new appointments. But other managers and workers—as well as some outside observers—did not think that the period had been an untypical one. Expanding productive capacity, changing processes and personnel, and new models, could not validly be said to have been exceptional in themselves or to have presented unfamiliar problems. More conclusive refutation of the view that the field-work was done during an 'unrepresentative' period may be found in the factory's long post-war history of labour discontent. The period of field-work was not an unusual one in terms of labour unrest—either by repute or by reference to official strike statistics.

The first part of this paper, then, describes what may be thought of as the anatomy of almost any car factory and the kind of work which car assembly entails. The structure of the management and labour organisation, and the procedural machinery for regulating industrial relations, are specific to the factory while yet having many features common to other car factories. In the second part, attention is concentrated on the physiology and actual functioning of this machinery and its parts: the sections present a typical shop stewards' meeting, some small and bigger strikes, and a top-level conference between management and trade unions on the state of the factory's industrial relations. Part III is a summing up, with some concluding remarks.

B   The Working Environment (1)

Cars are made very much the same way in all of the main assembly factories. The firm to which this study relates must remain unidentified,
and because there are relatively few car-assembly factories in the Midlands—or in the country as a whole—the paper deliberately sets up certain hazards for the amateur detective. Care has been taken to make
these hazards (mainly of nomenclature) of no importance to the purpose
of this study: their sole function is to disguise.

First impressions of the factory from the outside are forbidding. There
is a security system of high fences, few gates, and uniformed custodians—
presenting almost a military or penal aspect. Through the gates pass a
stream of trucks bringing supplies, car-transporters carrying body-
shells in and completed vehicles out, and a two-way movement of new
cars themselves—bearing the red licence plates required for short road
tests. Once inside the gates, several features cannot help but stand out
to the casual visitor or newcomer. The premises are relatively new:
there is little crumbling brickwork to be seen. In some areas there is
inevitably a good deal of oil about. At closer quarters the factory is not
generally noisy although there are obviously noisy areas like the body
shop. Under the main roofs there is mostly a low-volume but high-pitched
and characteristic noise—the weird, intermittent shriek of pneumatic
spanners and drills which is a constant accompaniment of car-assembly
work. The low rumble of the moving tracks is seldom audible. The
dominant smell of assembly areas is not of paint or swarf but of rubber
and plastics and oil, mingled with exhaust fumes from works' traffic.

The factory floor has a network of freeways for wheeled traffic, and a
wary eye and ear must always be kept open for this mechanical handling
equipment. Hand trucks and the physical manhandling of products are
mainly to be seen in areas of confined space where fork-lift trucks would
be impractical or where only short distances are involved. The assembly
areas themselves actually look like those stylised flow charts drawn by
work-study men. The activities taking place can be easily seen and com-
prehended—functions both of the size and general familiarity of the product being made. The flow of work is logical and perceptible, even though
the tracks themselves move fairly slowly. From one direction come
body-shells, moving through the processes of washing and de-greasing,
sealing, priming, rubbing and flatting, then painting again. They are oven-
dried, and then move onto conveyors which are lined on both sides with

_____

(1) Some parts of this section give a summary version of material in
     Labour Relations in the Motor Industry.

stores of hard components and soft 'trim'. These tracks then merge with another major flow line: engine and transmission units have been brought together and now travel along similar conveyors. The trimmed bodies are now hoisted and then lowered onto the power-transmission skeletons. The car continues along one main conveyor for accretion of the remaining bits and pieces, for wheels, washing, tuning, testing, and final inspection.

Inspection and documentary checks are made at many points along the tracks: pieces of paper and coloured card accumulate as an essential part of the assembly process. The rest of the production layout is supplementary to this main flow—sub-assembly lines for such items as engines, gearboxes, and consoles. There are trim shops for making seats and other items of interior trim; brass, polishing, and plating shops for making a variety of chromed parts; and a woodworking department. Taken together, the work processes make for neither boring incomprehensibility nor esoteric mystique about the making of cars. Nor are all 'staff' employees isolated from the physical aspects of production. Clerks and typists are peppered about the works, although the physical and social separation of most of the white-collar workers is real enough.

The range of actual jobs is, of course, wide despite the fact that there is very little of the fine and intricate work typical, for example, of the assembly of instruments. This kind of part—like speedometer clocks and other dashboard fittings, petrol pumps and carburettors—is bought from suppliers in a fully-assembled condition. Nor is there much heavy manual work of the kind associated with, for instance, metal manufacture. Even the sweeping and cleaning of the premises tends to be mechanised. Fetching, carrying, lifting and stacking is carried out mainly with the use of fork-lift trucks, and this work is facilitated by the use of more or less standardised bins or stillages. The most numerous worker is, of course, the assembler: about three out of five of the manual or hourly-paid workers are fitters, finishers, and trimmers (although not all of these assemblers are line or track-workers). The traditional craftsmen are relatively few in number, and are found in experimental and development departments, in the toolroom, and in maintenance gangs. In addition to office workers, the factory 'staff' include chargehands and foremen who— together with departmental superintendents—are somewhat loosely referred to as 'supervision'. Other staff are the 'progress chasers', i.e. those who keep the documentary records and the production lines in phase and who keep a check on the stocks of supplies. Work-study engineers or ratefixers, and some inspectors, also have staff status.

Tracks are the symbol of car factories, and a word must be said about the organisation of track-work. The jobs vary from attaching cloth or plastic pieces with adhesives to fitting and bolting bumpers. Most of the work involves drilling holes and screwing, bolting, riveting, or clipping small parts together and to the body-shells. A planned number of operations must be completed within fixed lengths of track and the period of time during which the car occupies this space. The way the work is actually done is the result of a number of interrelated factors: the length of track, i.e. the number of work stations which are possible; the number of models which it is capable of handling; the number of men who can

12

work without hindering each other in the space available; and the number of operations each can perform at given track speeds. Despite these imperatives, the time cycles of sets of operations vary in practice from track to track and over time: few could be completed within three minutes or took more than half an hour. Frequent transfers to different assembly tracks or onto different sets of operations took place, and could reduce the 'pressure' of track-work on individuals.

However the sets of operations are apportioned amongst the assemblers, there are inevitable differences in the effort required. There are loose and tight jobs, and a work station 'team' sometimes shuffle operations about between themselves for reasons of both equity and convenience. Generally, however, trackmen work not so much speedily as steadily. There are breaks for personal needs, while additional breaks may often be 'earned' by speeding up the pace of work and 'working back down the line', or by having other members of the team 'pull the job in' during temporary absences. Longer absences are covered by a corps of 'floaters', i.e. operatives with considerable experience of the particular models who can take the place of an absentee for an hour or a week. Floater gangs vary in strength from summer to winter—from about four to about eight per cent of the track labour complement.

Despite the absence of a rigorous survey, it was possible to arrive at impressions of what appeared to be general attitudes to track work, and to 'job satisfaction'. Trackmen did not complain about the work they were doing, of fatigue or monotony. This was a little surprising in view of the considerable evidence[1]—both British and American—about the attitudes of car workers to assembly-line jobs, and of popular beliefs about this kind of work (which, plausibly, could be expected to have some 'feedback effect' on car workers themselves). There were, of course, spontaneous complaints about particular and more onerous jobs, such as those which involved manual manipulation of heavy welding machines, a dirty 'blacking' job on the final line, or a particularly 'tight' job of threading and connecting an electrical harness. One 'militant' and rather heavily-built shop steward had been given a set of operations which required considerable bending on his part which he regarded as a kind of deliberate unfairness akin to victimisation. But there appeared to be little dissatisfaction with track work as such. On the contrary, as will appear

---

(1) For example, C.R. Walker and R. Guest, Man on the Assembly Line (Cambridge, Mass: Harvard University Press, 1952), Ely Chinoy, Automobile Workers and the American Dream (New York: Doubleday, 1955), S. Wyatt and R. Marriott, A Study of Attitudes to Factory Work, Medical Research Council Special Report Series 292, (HMSO 1956), and W.A. Faunce, 'Automation and the Automobile Worker', in Social Problems VI, 1, 1958. See Robert Blauner Alienation and Freedom (Chicago: University of Chicago Press, 1964), for a summary of this literature. The most recent British study is J.H. Goldthorpe, 'Attitudes and Behaviour of Car Assembly Workers: a deviant Case and a Theoretical Critique'. British Journal of Sociology, September, 1966.

later in the paper, complaints were most numerous and most vigorous when the tracks stopped moving—and the much lower 'waiting-time' rates of pay applied. No one spoke of such pauses providing a breathing space to offset monotony, exhaustion or emotional strain: the level of earnings seemed the major concern.

The involuntary changes in the pace of work, or the work-load, affected both trackmen and workers on a time basis of payment, such as store-men and internal transport drivers. In the case of trackmen, the expected levels of earnings were obtained when a 'target' number of vehicles had passed along the line each day. The pace of work could be varied by management either by altering the speed of the tracks or the spacing of the cars, and both methods were used to smooth out fluctuations in the flow process or to make up for periods when the tracks had stopped moving. This 'stop-go' production was resented by some men when it was thought to be due to management's inability to plan and operate a smooth production flow. In the case of day-workers, there seemed also to be very little dissatisfaction with the general nature of their work—which was no more than comparative research(1) would lead one to expect. What did cause complaint, amongst storemen for example, were un-scheduled increases in the work load—especially when these increases tended to coincide with decreases in the level of earnings. This point is taken up again in one of the case studies.

It is dangerous to generalise about feelings of insecurity. But in relation to employment and earnings such feelings did seem widespread. For example, short-time working and fluctuating earnings very often arose as topics in conversations which were conducted for any length of time. Although the factory had experienced no large-scale redundancies since 1956, over half the manual labour force had had less than five years' service there, and three quarters had been employed for less than ten years (as against two-thirds for another rapidly-growing firm for which comparable information is available). Labour turnover was not high (10 per cent in the year before the study), and rapid growth of the firm would seem to be the main explanation for what is probably a relatively low average length of service. But the factory had absorbed workers declared redundant by other motor firms during 1960 and 1961, and many individuals spoke readily of their experiences of redundancy. For ex-ample, senior stewards are generally long inhabitants of a factory: at this one the conveners had an average length of service with the firm of just under eleven years. Yet five out of six of these conveners had (at least since the end of the War) been made redundant at the firms for which they had worked. The other convener had been forewarned of a redundancy and had left at his own request. Although not all these firms had been in the motor industry, redundancy was recognised to be, and spoken of as, an important hazard of the industry. Management could use it as a weapon: at an 'emergency' meeting called by stewards' conven-ers with 'higher management', the final statement made by the Works

---

(1) See, for example, Robert Blauner, 'Work Satisfaction and Industrial Trends in Modern Society' in Labour and Trade Unionism ed. by Lipset and Galenson (New York: Wiley, 1960).

Manager to try and induce the withdrawal of an overtime ban by one section was that 'the firm would have to raise a redundancy list'.

It is noteworthy that very few men spoke or complained about the motor industry as such, or said that they had thought about the possibility of leaving it. Some men who had recently come to the factory from other car firms did not like the move, and spoke rather wistfully of their chances of returning to the other firms. There was for several weeks an efflux which mildly alarmed both management and one of the conveners (whose members seemed to be disproportionately concerned in this movement). The factory was said to have had a bad reputation for working conditions and labour relations generally, although the level of earnings for a full or normal working week compared favourably with other car factories in the area. What seemed at the root of the unrest during the period was chronic but irregular short-time working—as will be discussed in detail later. What is of note here is that there seemed to be an acceptable level of insecurity, and that resentment became vociferous or active only when this level increased sharply. It has been suggested that the high earnings of workers in the British car industry are a major form of compensation for this irregularity and insecurity of employment, and that car workers bargain aggressively in good times to make up for their 'losses' in the bad times. The suggestion seems both logical and plausible, and fits in with things workers in the factory spoke about.(1)

Pay was, of course, the major focus of working interest. Before indicating the range and amounts of pay packets, it is possible to say something about the relation between pay and work pace. The general tempo or speed at which people in the factory worked seemed to cluster about three rough norms. Individual piece-workers, such as welders on body-making, trimmers on seat or console making, or lathe operators, tended to move observably faster than both the trackmen and those who 'serviced' the tracks—such as storemen, for example. The difference was expected, imposed, and roughly standardised: jobs paid by the piece are planned to exhibit a 'piece-work effort' or performance about one-third greater than 'day-work effort'—and with higher rates of pay. The trackmen—on a bonus payment system—work less speedily than piece-workers, but their pace is, of course, relatively closely governed. The trackmen's pace of work can vary according to the looseness or tightness of the specific sets of operations, the possibilities of working down or back the line, according to slight variations in line speeds during the day to adjust for bottlenecks or shortages, and finally, according to the possibilities which some trackmen have to build 'banks' of sub-assemblies which they can then draw on if they wish to slow their pace of work for a time. The mechanical pacing of the track also partly governs the overall pacing of the day-workers who service them. However, the nature and expected pace of daywork allows greater variability of effort: two or more hours could often be 'freed' by building 'banks' or—more dangerously—

_____

(1) The suggestion was made by Geoffrey Roberts, and has been discussed at greater length in Labour Relations in the Motor Industry.

by working harder to catch up on borrowed time. Day-workers are thus seldom rushed, even allowing for different patterns of individual self-pacing. In short, individual piece-work is highly-paced and fairly continuous, track-work is slower but more constant, while day-work need seldom raise a sweat.

Car workers are not all highly paid, and rates of pay and earnings vary greatly both between occupations and for the same individual over the weeks. In this factory, the most noticeable occupational differences in earnings were those between day-workers and piece-workers. Day-workers formed about one in five of all hourly-paid employees at the works. Of these, storemen were the largest single occupational group, other day-workers being labourers, internal transport drivers, material handlers, and so on. At this time, day-workers' pay ranged from about 4s. 5d. per hour in the case of labourers to about 7s. in the case of some hourly-paid inspectors. With the addition of an output bonus based on the number of cars completed at the works, and with a small amount of overtime working, a storeman could be expected to earn between £14 and £16 a week—the range of day-workers' average weekly earnings being from about £12 to £20. However, the weekly bonus element could fluctuate between a few shillings and about £5—and this variation often had little connection with the work-load of day-workers themselves. A number of disputes which centred on these bonus fluctuations are discussed later in the paper.

Most of the individual piece-workers were welders, metal mechanics, and sheet metal workers who worked on body-shells, radiator grilles and other small metal parts. Piece-work earnings for a full week varied between £25 and £28. The trackmen's payments-by-results system was organised to yield them about £25 to £26 in a normal week for an agreed or target work load. Paintshop workers earned slightly more and final line workers slightly less. As in the case of day-workers, the trackmen's 'bonus' formed a substantial proportion of 'normal' earnings: variations in work flow, and in the amount of 'waiting time'(1) produced large fluctuations in their earnings from week to week, quite apart from the effects of strikes and lay-offs. For example, the earnings of trackmen on the final line were sometimes over £30, frequently below £20, and sometimes even under £15 a week. For a few years prior to this study, trackmen did work regular overtime during the spring and early summer, three quarters of an hour overtime for three nights a week being the usual arrangement. But they did not work overtime during the period of the study and could not make up the potential earnings foregone due to short-time working and waiting-time. During this period only the final line-workers were on regular overtime, and they were paid an agreed temporary 'lieu' rate—because of the unusually irregular production flow and large number of inspection 'rejects'.

The factory had a patchwork of bonus systems, all of which had the number of cars produced each week as the basic ingredient. Trackmen's

---

(1) Waiting time was an issue in a dispute recounted later, and will be discussed there.

bonus generally depended on the number of cars traversing their line, but was influenced also by the labour loading (as reflected in the aggregate number of hours worked by the workers on that line). The day-workers' bonus schemes depended on the number of cars completed at the works, as well as by the labour loading of the particular department and the number of hours worked (overtime counted as a penalty element). There was a separate bonus scheme embracing management executives below Director level and all monthly-paid staff. The firm had no salary grading scheme for 'staff': an offer of employment would specify a salary with a built-in bonus element calculated at the then normal or planned production level, because the management bonus was based entirely on the output of completed cars. Target production gave a bonus element which formed a substantial proportion of total salary. Few managers would discuss their salary—but the system seemed to be resented. Weekly-paid staff—including typists, clerks, comptometer and punch operators, tracers and some drawing-office staff—had, through their unions, the year before successfully objected to the bonus scheme and were now paid fixed salaries.

Printed 'Works Rules' were handed to each hourly-paid worker when he began his employment at the firm. These rules gave information about the working hours, breaks, shift arrangements, time-keeping, movement passes, deductions from pay, reduced pay for faulty work, disputes procedure, the guaranteed week, redundancy arrangements, and so on. The booklet had been printed some years before and much of the information was out of date: it was an inadequate guide either to the current rules or to actual practice. The current works rules were subject to approved departmental variation, and a further modification or 'loose interpretation' of the rules in practice which varied according to the nature of the rule and the department concerned, as well as between points of time. The standards of enforcement were not consistently applied. For example, speed limits for works vehicles, and one-way traffic signs on works roads, were only very occasionally insisted upon by the works police. Many drivers of works vehicles did not have the written 'permits' specified by rule.

Other examples of 'flexible' works rules may be given.

The morning tea-break was officially of ten minutes duration, whereas in some departments supervisors would accept a break of up to twenty minutes. While there was no official tea-break in the afternoon, tea could be taken while work continued. In practice, anticipating the tea trolleys and queuing on their arrival made a break almost ubiquitous. 'Washing up' time at the end of the day was longer than that specified by rule. Again, despite the rules prohibiting the practice, workers did 'clock on' for each other, both for reasons of convenience and to cover lateness (there was no 'clocking off' at this factory except for those who obtained permission to leave the premises early, or who worked overtime). Supervisors knew of this, and accepted it. On the other hand, some works rules were strictly applied: passouts to leave the factory during working hours had to be produced to the 'blue-bottles' (as the Works Police were called) at the factory gates. No smoking was permitted in certain areas—for reasons of safety. Yet works rules—despite their imprecise definition and erratic application—seldom gave rise to problems at shop-floor level.

Prescribed methods or systems of working were often disregarded. Workers sometimes said that, in their view, rules had to be broken to get the job done. On occasion, this attitude could best be interpreted as mere resistance to change, as when a new bin identification system was introduced in the spare parts stores and was, on balance, superior to the old method. The new system was fully adopted only after transfer (for other reasons) had removed the older workers from that section. In some cases the breach of regulations saved time or trouble but carried just the hazards rules were designed to avoid. For example, the use of stepladders could be avoided in some stores by what was know as the 'monkey trick', which was more convenient but could fairly easily lead to injury. But there were also a host of 'productivity wrinkles'—such as the knack of inserting piston rings into cylinder blocks without using the jigs provided; or by skillfully drilling holes in two or more components at a time when the official method specified that they be done singly. One of the workers summed up this kind of strategem rather appropriately: 'If you want to know the most efficient way to do a job, give it for a month or two to the laziest man in the gang'.

This raises questions about works discipline. Sanctions and discipline intrude themselves perhaps less in car factories than in other places of work: moving tracks enforce their own supervision—of work-pace if not of work quality. In situations where every operation can be attributed to an individual worker (or for which a particular individual could be held responsible), and where succeeding operations often depend on the satisfactory completion of work only a short distance 'back down the line', inspection and quality are partially ensured by the technology as well as by the informal supervision which men may exercise over each other. Some foremen supervised more than a hundred trackmen each, and their tasks were made up largely of problems of labour-loading due to absenteeism and transfers, changes in cycles of operations, sudden crises due to non-standard parts, mechanical failure, and so on. Constant surveillance or 'bossing about' was neither necessary nor in evidence.

Workers' relations with their supervisors were a function of both general forces and individual quirks. Competence and ability were soon mutually recognised and respected. Work allocated by an able foreman could be accepted and carried out willingly, whereas a less able supervisor could face more difficulties and fuss in getting the same tasks completed. Grumbles were related sometimes to the person of the supervisor rather than to the content of the job to be done. But overlying these personal considerations was the large area of expected or customary workshop behaviour between workers and supervisors. Infringements of many works rules were acceptable to supervisors provided they were made unobtrusively—thus allowing a supervisor some defence against higher authority. In the stores, for example, men could not sit down or look as though they had nothing to do—even if this was true. 'Other business' could be conducted without interference if a stores document was being 'consulted'. Walking and talking had to be 'with intent' (as the work study officers who examined the stores described it).

The 'cover' was spurious and formed the cloak of a kind of tacit conspiracy. Like swearing (the vocabularies being overworked and rather monotonous), these things were examples of an elaborate role-playing ritual of work relations which seemed to be sloughed off like dustcoats at the end of the day.

Personal or direct contact with higher levels of supervision is for most workers infrequent: even within departments there was seldom any face-to-face relation with the superintendent or manager. And outside the immediate area of work, status was diffused by problems of personal identification. There was latitude in the choice of factory uniform—although this was less so for management than for workers. For example, storemen voluntarily wore brown dustcoats made available by the firm at cost price and paid for by deductions from wages. Blue boiler suits were common in engine assembly areas and the paint shops. Trackmen wore no uniform, and many of them did not wear protective clothing at all as the work is generally clean. Military characteristics were almost mandatory in the dress of lower management. Supervisors wore brown or white coats with different colour edging to the collars to denote their particular function or status. But inspectors—whether they were 'staff' or hourly-paid—and rate-fixers also wore white coats ungarnished with edging. Superintendents wore suits—the unambiguous working dress of middle and senior management.

A worker's ability to move about the premises was a measure of 'induction'. Sanctions could be applied for short absences from a workplace only by the supervision of that department, and in practice these could sometimes be forestalled by an informal word with the junior foreman beforehand. In a factory of several thousand workers, personal anonymity could be achieved at quite a short distance from the workplace, and workers could move about at will outside their own departments—provided they took the precaution of acting 'with intent' and were familiar with the layout and jargon of the factory. Trackmen were by virtue of their work fairly restricted in their geographical movements, but many other workers were required to move about outside the area of direct supervision. Perhaps the most important single factor in setting the level of geographical freedom for those at a fixed workplace was just this necessary coming and going by others—including the more permanent changes resulting from labour turnover.

Personal anonymity was evidence of a much more important characteristic of the factory. There was a surprising 'compartmentalisation' of interest and attitude. Car workers as such have not produced a solid or distinct vocational community akin to that of miners or dockers, and this was very evident even inside the factory. For example, the workers in one department or store would know very little about events taking place in contiguous departments. The workers' lines of communication in this context were primitive—and seemed to depend on chance or haphazard contacts between individuals in different departments. Interest in other departments as such was very limited. For example, workshop meetings taking place during working hours and in full view of neighbouring departments called for no comment from these latter—not even from their departmental stewards even when questioned by the author.

These things indicated that a sense of solidarity amongst workers in the factory was of a tenuous, limited, or even grudging kind. There were attitudes or feelings not merely of apathy but of antipathy towards other groups of workers—most clearly evident in the division between day-workers and trackmen. Day-workers—as has been indicated—earned much less than trackmen, and depended on an output bonus and overtime working for what they considered a living wage. When trackmen stopped work, the output-linked bonus fell off for all, and—because component deliveries were then diverted into stores rather than direct to track stations—the workload of at least some day-workers increased at these times whilst for many it remained more or less the same. Knowledge of trackmen's earnings was widespread and accurate; trackmen worked little or no overtime; and their skills were not held to justify the earnings differential. Trackmen could thus easily be held to be 'irresponsible': they were envied and unpopular at the same time. Many day-workers stated that they felt that trackmen were unsympathetic to the problems of the day-workers, and that trackmen would be unwilling to support day-workers in disputes. Day-workers' shop stewards complained on several occasions in this vein at the regular general meetings of shop stewards, and on balance it did seem that their grievances received less attention at the time than they seemed to warrant—perhaps not wholly on account of pressure of other events.

There were conflicts of interest also between track departments themselves. For example, due to irregular work flow, the final line had negotiated the temporary 'lieu' rate of payment already referred to. When the flow of work had steadied again, the final line workers pressed to return to the previous payment system—and staged a series of minor stoppages and overtime bans to hasten the change. Other trackmen were sent home on some of these occasions—management said that this was a necessary consequence of the 'irresponsible' bans and stoppages, while some workers said it was in reprisal, or because sales had fallen off and the cars were not required. These matters will be considered again later, but here it need only be noted that the knowledge of other men being laid off work was insufficient to persuade the final line workers to desist from their actions. The Factory's Industrial Relations Officer—who had himself been a leading shop steward—held that it was not only the final line workers who behaved in 'a selfish manner' to get what they could for themselves, but other departmental groups as well. However, this 'compartmentalised' aspect can be over-emphasised. It likens the factory to a cluster of virtually autonomous productive cells linked in a symbiotic relationship, and detracts attention from the wider bases of organisation. The next three sections provide an account of the factory's collective organisations—of management and workers—and of the joint machinery for the regulation of their relations.

C   Industrial Relations Machinery: Management

The firm's activities were confined to the production of motor vehicles, and the assembly factory which forms the subject of this study was only one of a group of establishments under the control of a board of executive directors. The Group Director was chairman of the board, while the other directors were each in charge of specific aspects of the firm's operations. For example, the Technical Manager was the board member who was responsible for the design and development of bodies and engines; while directors with more self-explanatory functions were the Sales Manager, the Chief Accountant, and the Chief Buyer. On the other hand, managerial responsibility for industrial relations matters was less precisely allocated. Although the Group Director had formally placed the final responsibility for negotiations with workers and their trade unions in the hands of another board member—the Works Manager—in practice the Group Director sometimes became personally and immediately involved in these matters, as when—without reference to shop-floor management or shop stewards—he approached and addressed a meeting of inspectors who were discussing the progress of negotiations over a bonus scheme, or when the posting and particular wording of a Works Notice were the subject of dispute. Full-time trade union officials would also, on occasion, negotiate directly with the Group Director (as will be apparent later).

Another member of the board of directors who had formal responsibility for an area of industrial relations functions was the Production Manager. The Works Manager was in charge of production departments, while the Production Manager was more concerned with planning. The Production Manager was, inter alia, in charge of the Work Study Department, the main tasks of which were the negotiation of piece-work prices at shop floor level and the development and application of production bonus schemes. Also, because production scheduling featured prominently in many labour disputes, the Production Manager was usually present at meetings between 'higher management' and senior shop stewards. A personal factor may also have been at work: the Production Manager was a board member of longer standing than the Works Manager, and it seemed to an outside observer that at joint meetings with the shop stewards at which both directors were present, the Production Manager had the more senior status and spoke with greater authority. This 'informal' influence on labour relations—like that of the Group Director—should be borne in mind when looking at the abbreviated outline of the formal management organisation (Illustration I). However, the main point of note here is that the firm, at this time, had no director or senior manager whose sole or even main function was the conduct or coordination of

Illustration I

ABBREVIATED OUTLINE OF MANAGEMENT ORGANISATION

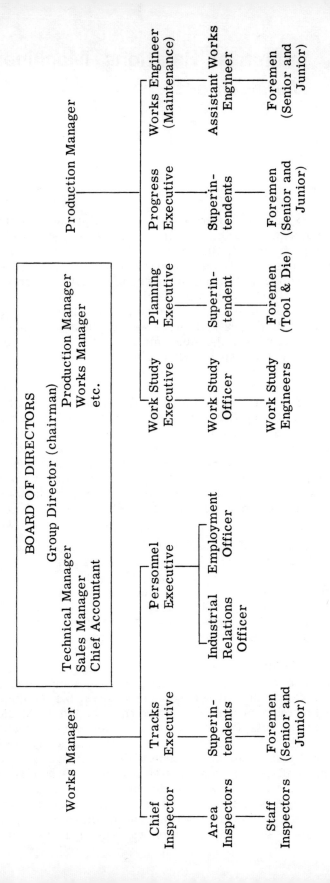

negotiations or of industrial relations matters generally. Neither the Personnel Executive nor the Industrial Relations Officer were members of senior management.

The other levels of management may be briefly described: the middle layer was occupied by a number of 'executives', for example, Stores Executive—in charge of the physical movement and placing of supplies; Machine Shop Executive—in charge of engine assembly and testing (a function which was being transferred to another factory during the study); Works Engineer—in charge of factory maintenance; Chief Draughtsman; Chief Inspector, etc. The superintendents were immediately under the control of the executives, and were responsible for more specific and limited functions. They were at the apex of the hierarchy of 'supervision'. This was a loosely-used term, but applied in practice to the 'lower' or 'junior' levels of management. A superintendent was in charge of a particular workshop or department, and had a number of foremen of senior and junior grade reporting to him. Superintendents could refuse to employ a worker recommended by the Personnel Department, and could dismiss workers in their departments. They determined the composition of working teams or gangs, and allocated work between them. The junior foremen were the front-line supervisors: there were no positions of chargehand or leading hand between junior foremen and workers.

As there was no explicit or agreed system of salary grading, the range of earnings for any level of management—or for persons carrying comparable titles—was said to be wide. For the higher levels, the information available allows for no more than guestimates. For example, the directors were thought to receive annual salaries ranging from £3,500 to £10,000 and more—excluding directors' fees. Executives—depending on their length of service and span of responsibility—were paid between £1,750 and about £4,000 a year, while superintendents were paid from £1,500 to £1,750. Senior foremen received about £29 a week, and junior foremen about £26—although in at least one department this latter figure was only about £22. All of the salaries referred to above included the production bonuses—which were calculated on the basis of the total number of cars completed each week. The bonus element formed a large part of the salary and management earnings could vary accordingly.

The two departments which had industrial relations as their basic concern were both to some extent in a 'transitional' and unsettled state. The first of these was the Work Study Department, which consisted of a number of 'work study engineers' under a superintendent and executive who reported to the Production Manager. Before the appointment of a new executive during the period, there had been little rigorous work study in the sense that job methods and content were not determined by reference to time and motion study. The work study engineers were in practice rate-fixers and effort-bargainers. For example, when the work content of payment-by-results workers was radically altered, an agreed experimental rate would be set—which might apply for a period as long as six months—after which the new set of operations would be timed by the rate-fixer, using a stopwatch and in the presence of the selected workers' shop stewards. The haggling would then begin, on the basis of how the earnings 'yield' on rates being suggested or demanded would compare with the level of earnings of others in the department who were doing comparable work. In the case of piece-workers, the haggling would be about the number of 'pieces' to be produced in a given period. In the case of trackmen, however—where there were no 'pieces'—the equivalent was the set or cycle of particular operations, and the bargaining in these cases was about the actual operations or work content rather than the number of sets of operations to be done. Rate-fixing was essentially a bargaining process—spoken of as such by the Work Study Engineers and their immediate superiors.

The Work Study Department was responsible for preparing and assisting in the negotiation of the various bonus schemes. These were based on the output of cars, and as this was outside the control of day-workers there was little or no 'incentive' in the schemes for these workers—in the sense that increased effort on their part could not clearly be seen to produce more cars and thus higher earnings. But the schemes did contain an effort-bargain. They were mostly being applied on a departmental basis: a bonus sum for each car produced was paid into the departmental 'bonus pool' which had then to be shared by workers in the department. The shares were affected by the labour-loading, i.e. the number of workers in the department, by absenteeism, and by the aggregate hours worked by men in the department. The acceptance of fewer men to do the work of the department, doing the work of absentees without applying for a replacement, and keeping overtime working to a minimum, would all raise the shares of bonus which each worker received.

An example of the form which this kind of bargaining took can be briefly outlined. The spares storemen were dissatisfied with the fluctuations in their bonus earnings, and pressed for a scheme which would relate bonus earnings more closely to their own efforts. The actual events are given in one of the case studies. The Work Study Department examined work in the stores, using techniques such as activity sampling and work-flow analysis, reported that the stores were overmanned, and recommended that several men be transferred to other departments. The resultant bargaining was about whether the work could be done with a reduced labour complement, and by how much such reductions would increase the share of the weekly bonus pool which each remaining storeman would receive. In this case, the more fundamental cause of discontent—big fluctuations in bonus earnings—was not affected, and continued to give rise to problems. However, the new Work Study Executive was unhappy both about rate-fixing and about effort bargaining of this kind, and spoke of introducing more rigorous time, method, and motion study into the factory.

The other department intimately concerned with industrial relations was, of course, the Personnel Department. The division of functions in the Department was not unusual: the Employment Officer and his assistants handled the 'bread and butter' personnel matters such as recruitment or screening, transfers, and general record-keeping for all employees, while the Personnel Executive arranged and took part in negotiations with both hourly-paid and white-collar workers' representatives, and was in overall charge of the Department. A Safety Officer (for the firm) also reported directly to the Personnel Executive, but there were no general or centralised training arrangements—and thus no training officers. However, during an early stage in the field-work for this study, the firm offered the new post of Industrial Relations Officer to one of the leading shop stewards at the factory—an offer which was accepted. An inter-departmental notice attributed the appointment to the continued expansion of the firm, but a number of other reasons were also in circulation. One of these was the chronically strike-prone pattern of industrial relations at the factory. Individuals spoke of a lack of confidence on the part of both shop stewards and some managers in the overall adequacy of the Personnel Department in general, the functioning of which was hampered also by ill-health of the Personnel Executive. Again, other car firms were strengthening their industrial relations staffs, and there were precedents for appointing shop stewards to these positions. There was also the suggestion that the firm was only 'buying out' a dangerous adversary —but this sort of explanation was bound to arise under the circumstances.

The new Industrial Relations Officer was made 'responsible for industrial relations, which form a part of the functions of the Personnel Department'—a statement which, because of its general terms, indicated the initially unsettled position of his office. It was not for some weeks after his appointment took effect that his formal responsibilities and role in the factory's procedure for settling labour disputes were defined. It was thought by some shop stewards and managers at the time of his appointment that he would at some not-too-distant date replace the Personnel Executive: a suspicion that was strengthened by his almost immediate assumption of many of the major functions of the Personnel Executive— the arrangement of and participation in the negotiations involving hourly-paid workers. The novelty of his appointment was an important factor in one of the strikes discussed later, and even after this particular dispute had been settled, resentments, and an unsettled atmosphere remained in the Personnel Department—as well, of course, as in the shop steward organisation—because of his previous position. The next section describes the labour organisation at the factory, and some of the effects of the change in personnel.

D   Industrial Relations Machinery: Labour

The firm was a member of the local Engineering Employers' Association, was therefore federated to the national Engineering Employers' Federation and was party to the agreements between that body and the Confederation of Shipbuilding and Engineering Unions. Trade union organisation at the factory—like that in most of the other British car factories
—remained comparatively (in engineering terms) weak until the immediate post-war years. The firm had been unwilling to recognise trade
unionism: for example, in 1938 there was a week-long strike when metal
workers refused to sign an undertaking required by the firm making non-
membership of a trade union a condition of employment. Shop stewards
at the factory, and trade union officials in the area, spoke of the factory
having had a bad reputation for general working conditions and relations
with trade unions and shop stewards for a period extending well into the
1950's—and pointed to the dismissals of particular shop stewards. However, there seems little doubt that by about 1950, trade union organisation
at this factory had become almost complete. The factory's strike record
does reflect a period of turbulence during the half-dozen years after the
War, followed by half-a-dozen years of comparative calm—at least inso-
far as the public strike reports are concerned. And there is harder,
though indirect, evidence of strong factory organisation by this time: a
handbook of works regulations and conditions of employment (bearing the
dates 1949 and 1952) provided for a weekly meeting of shop stewards
'for which the Company provide facilities and pay the Shop Stewards concerned for one hour'. Also, 'Standing Orders' approved by the 'Confed-
erated Shop Stewards' Council' at the end of 1952 show the existence of
a fund 'raised by levy and collected by the Company... used to re-im-
burse stewards losing time on Union business'.

However, at the time of the study there seemed to be no non-trade unionists—'nonners'—amongst the hourly-paid workers at the factory, and the
white-collar unions were said to be steadily increasing their membership. Certainly it was not possible for a manual worker to obtain employment at the factory unless he was either a member of an 'appropriate'
trade union already, or unless he agreed to become a member within a
short (unspecified) time. There were six 'appropriate' unions at the factory: it is not possible to give exact membership figures, because not
only do the unions concerned not keep rigorous and up-to-date records
of this kind, but there were transfers of workers—mainly members of the
Amalgamated Engineering Union (A.E.U.)—to other plants during the
period. However, the Transport and General Workers, Union (T.G.W.U.)
and the National Union of Vehicle Builders (N.U.V.B.) were the largest—
each with about one third of all manual workers at the factory as members. The A.E.U. had come to have only about ten per cent, as a conse-

quence of the transfers already mentioned. The remainder were shared between the Birmingham and Midland Sheet Metal Workers' Society and the National Union of Sheet Metal Workers and Coppersmiths (which operated and were treated as one union—which can be called the S.M.W.U.) and the National Society of Metal Mechanics (N.S.M.M.). The smallest 'appropriate' union in the factory was the Amalgamated Society of Wood-cutting Machinists (A.S.W.M.)—some of whose members were engaged on work with metals.

Amongst the manual workers, there were thought to be about a dozen members of the Electrical Trades Union, five or six members of the National Union of General and Municipal Workers, and only two or three dozen men altogether who were members of yet other unions—not all of them engineering unions. These were men who had either been with the firm for a long time, or who were in the process of changing unions—a process which could take a long time depending on the zeal of shop stewards and branch officials. A 'Preferential Shop' was operated at the factory. There was an understanding between conveners and the management that in good times there was a union shop, and in bad times a closed shop, i.e. while the appropriate unions had members on their vacant books and these were available and suitable, no members of other unions or nonners would be employed. On the white-collar side, the only comparable situation was that for draughtsmen—who were all members of the Draughtsmen's and Allied Technicians' Association (D.A.T.A.). Not more than about two-thirds of the clerical and supervisory grades were members of trade unions, the largest of which—in terms of membership in the factory—was the National Association of Clerical and Supervisory Staffs, i.e. the white-collar section of the T.G.W.U. The Clerical and Administrative Workers' Union had only about half the membership of N.A.C.S.S. There may have been members of other white-collar unions at the factory, but information on this point is not available.(1)

There were some areas or departments which were recognised as the preserve of one or other of the appropriate trade unions. For example, the toolroom workers were all A.E.U. members, whilst the polishing departments employed N.S.M.M. members with the exception of one T.G.W.U. member. On the other hand, some occupations in the factory were the preserve of a particular union, for example, welders—who were employed in the body shop, the brass shop, and in the service department —were members of the S.M.W.U. But the body shop as an area was shared between the S.M.W.U. and the N.U.V.B., and the brass shop between the S.M.W.U., the A.E.U., the T.G.W.U., and the A.S.W.M. Some large departments were effectively reserved for particular unions: the paint shops were the preserve of the T.G.W.U., and the trim shops the preserve of the N.U.V.B. In fact, there were about twenty T.G.W.U.

---

(1) There was very little contact between manual and white-collar union representatives at the factory—even between those of the T.G.W.U. and N.A.C.S.S. For example, one of the more senior conveners—who had held office in the factory's shop steward organisation for over ten years—revealed at one meeting that he did not know what 'D.A.T.A.' referred to in a letter he had received.

members in the trim shops, and a dozen N.U.V.B. men in the paint shops: mostly men who had been with the firm for some years. Their presence caused no problems partly because there was an understanding between the conveners that as these men left the firm or were transferred, their places would be taken by members of the 'appropriate' union for each department.

In most of the assembly or track departments, trade union membership was fairly mixed, and transfers of men between these departments could take place without regard to union membership. Storemen and some other day-workers could also belong to any of the main unions in the fac-tory—although most of these workers were in fact members of the T.G.W.U. In these mixed-union departments the particular union to which a worker belonged was not of importance to his fellow workers or even to his shop steward in most cases. What was important was that he should be a trade union member. However, in at least some of the mixed departments, there did seem to be a continuing trend towards the growth of single-union departments. For example, one assembly-line in a new building had a heavy concentration of N.U.V.B. members—who were in-terested in 'closing this shop', while one section of the final line in the same building had become closed to all but T.G.W.U. members. In an-other assembly department the number of A.E.U. members had been steadily declining while N.U.V.B. membership had been increasing. In this case, union pressures were not the only explanation: 'finishers'—who were N.U.V.B. members—had a basic rate (or Consolidated Time Rate) of almost 2d per hour more than 'fitters'—who were A.E.U. members. Fit-ters unobtrusively changed union to obtain the higher rate, while the shop superintendent would also ask for finishers rather than fitters when recruiting or replacing men because they were prepared—and allowed by other workers—to perform a greater range of operations.

But in general, inter-union rivalry for members and for work had become largely contained or settled by agreement and understandings about tra-ditional—almost accidental—spheres of interest. Trade union affairs as such were clearly of less immediate importance to most workers than the issues which arose in their own particular departments—whether these were of mixed or 'closed' union membership. Very few workers attended even irregularly their union branch meetings—even when the branches were organised on a workplace rather than a geographical basis (as was the case with the T.G.W.U. factory branch).(1) This is not to say that the underlying or latent inter-union tensions were not some-times in evidence in the relations between some shop stewards, or that the establishment of new departments or altered plant layouts did not occasionally bring these tensions to the surface for a time. Stewards would occasionally express private doubts about the intentions of other unions than their own, either as organisations or in the persons of their representatives, but it could be expected that such inter-union rivalry as existed would be more apparent within the shop steward hierarchy than amongst the ordinary membership.

---

(1) The S.M.W.U. was said to have good attendances at branch meetings, and to actually impose fines for absence without good cause.

The system of workers' representation was on a departmental basis. In theory, each department elected its shop stewards once a year—usually by a show of hands at a lunch-hour meeting called for the purpose. In practice, the process was untidy. Like full-time officials, shop stewards —having been elected—tended to remain in office. This was not a demonstration of the 'iron law of oligarchy', for shop stewards' positions were unpaid and carried few priviliges. The control or influence of many stewards over their electorate was very limited or even non-existent, and there was an ingrained fear of reprisal or dismissal attached to the role. The stewards were under pressure from both management and their own men, and a consideration of the case studies which follow will make it clear why few candidates were said to present themselves for election. It is probable that the elections were mostly a formality—and certain that they were sometimes dispensed with. Lists of accredited stewards —i.e. men recognised as such by both management and their trade unions —showed few changes. Conveners spoke of the problem in some departments of finding sufficient candidates to ensure adequate representation, while a number of stewards, when asked why they stood for election, replied that 'there was nobody else willing to take on the job'. Allowing for the normal canons of modesty and understatement, it was clear that there was in general little rivalry for the positions of ordinary or departmental shop steward. For conveners' positions, there was more competition (as will be discussed below).

There were no formal rules about the number of stewards to represent particular departments, the minimum number of workers required for representation or additional representation, or about minimum or maximum qualifications required by candidates presenting themselves for election. Shop-floor democracy was free of constitutional provisions of this kind, and, as this would lead one to expect, there were wide variations in the density of representation both over the years and as between departments and between unions. For example, minute books of the Joint Shop Stewards' Council (as it then was) for 1953 indicated that there was probably—on average for the factory as a whole—only one shop steward for about every 100 workers. By the time of the study there was an accredited shop steward for every 45-50 workers.

The extent of this increase in the density of workers' representation at the factory may have been exaggerated slightly by a temporary running down of the labour force and transfers of men between factories at the time of the study. A general explanation for the increase lies in the growth of workplace bargaining since the war, while more specific suggestions offered at the factory attributed the increase in density to pressure exerted by conveners and full-time officials as the expansion of the factory created many new departments. But an average figure of this kind in any case conceals wide variations between departments. For example, for the Tool Stores there was one steward for only eleven men— a density matched only by the Dispatch Department. At the other extreme, the engine assembly and test sections had only one steward per 150 men—this low density being a direct result of the transfers of men already referred to. The experimental and development departments were sited at several different parts of the factory, employed altogether 100 men, and shared only one steward between them. The more usual situation, however, was where large and compact departments each had a labour force measured in the hundreds—as in the paint shops, trim shops, and assembly areas: here there was an unwritten understanding that one steward for between 35 and 45 men allowed for reasonable representation.

The T.G.W.U. and the N.U.V.B. had 30 and 27 shop stewards respectively, while the number of A.E.U. stewards at the factory had dwindled to 10. The N.S.M.M. and the A.S.W.M. had 3 accredited stewards each. The above five unions had on average between 40 and 50 members represented by each shop steward. The remaining manual workers' union—the S.M.W.U.—had apparently about 80 members for each of three accredited shop stewards. This is a misleading figure partly because one of the three did not represent the union's members, and partly because the union had six additional 'committeemen' who had some shop steward functions at the departmental level, but who did not formally have the facilities which went with 'accreditation' (which will be noted later). The A.S.W.M. had also 2 additional but non-accredited representatives to attend to the interests of some members on permanent night-shift working. Regarding trade union representation on the staff side, both the N.A.C.S.S. and the Clerical and Administrative Workers' Union had each an accredited 'representative' at the factory. These representatives acted for all staff departments in which they had members—although the C.A.W.U. had, in addition, an 'assistant representative' who looked after members' interests in the Service Department only. D.A.T.A. also had an 'assistant representative' at the factory, but the leading representative of this union worked at another of the firm's factories. No adequate information is available on the numbers of members 'serviced' by the representatives of the white-collar unions.

The mixture of trade union members on the shop-floor in this (and other) car factories—and their 'transferability'—implies that many departmental shop stewards almost necessarily represent men who are not members of their own trade union. To this extent the figures for the average number of members of his own union represented by a shop steward may be misleading. In this factory, for example, not only did an A.E.U. steward in the brass shop represent members of at least three other unions, but there were four times as many members of the T.G.W.U. than there were A.E.U. members in the section—and they did not elect a T.G.W.U. steward. There were two or three other departments where, although there were sufficient members of a union to insist on separate representation by one of their number, the men elected stewards from other unions. For example, T.G.W.U. and N.U.V.B. members both accepted A.E.U. stewards on one assembly track, while N.U.V.B. and A.E.U. inspectors accepted representation by T.G.W.U. stewards. When asked specifically why this arrangement was acceptable to them, men replied that they supported the best (or sometimes the only) man available for the steward's job. Perhaps the best example demonstrating shop-floor respect for competence rather than trade union membership in the election of shop stewards was in a maintenanance department: the shop steward was said to be the only member of the S.M.W.U. amongst mainly A.E.U. and T.G.W.U. members. In this case, although 'accredited' by this union (as mentioned in the previous paragraph), he did not represent any of its members.

In addition to shop stewards, there were 'committeemen' of different kinds. Firstly, the stewards of each union formed a factory committee for that union. These committees (in the case of the main unions) in an abbreviated form, sometimes convened during working hours, on the premises and by permission of the management. 'Full'—though often poorly-attended—meetings of these factory committees were held periodically at the local trade union offices. Secondly, there were committees formed on a departmental basis, whose members need neither be accredited shop stewards nor all belong to the same trade union. For example, the 'Body Shop Committee' was composed of equal numbers of N.U.V.B. and S.M.W.U. members, only two of a total committee of eight members being accredited stewards. For the trim shops together there was a departmental committee of 22 men for 380 workers, but in this case they were made up of N.U.V.B. members only. Eight of the 22 were shop stewards. All of these committees had an ambiguous status: they were not formally recognised by the firm, although in practice they could sometimes receive facilities—from supervision at departmental level even if not from the Personnel Department. Committeemen who were not also stewards—were at the foot of the hierarchy of shop-floor trade union representation.

All the accredited shop stewards of all six manual workers' trade unions were automatically members of the factory's Joint Shop Stewards' Committee (J.S.S.C.). 'Congress' would perhaps have been a more appropriate appellation for this gathering of 76 men. The J.S.S.C. was recognised by the firm, had its own printed stationery, a bank account, and elected its office-bearers according to an agreed constitution—or 'Standing Orders'. One function of each of the main unions' factory committees was to elect from amongst its number a 'convener' and assistant convener for that union. (In the case of the smaller unions the conveners were elected by their entire memberships in the factory.) There were thus six conveners, who stood near the top of the shop steward hierarchy, and from amongst whose number the chairman, deputy-chairman, secretary, and treasurer of the J.S.S.C. had to be chosen by the J.S.S.C. Each office-bearer was elected for one year, but to maintain continuity, the elections were staggered—one office being vacated each quarter. Voting was by a show of hands. Under Standing Orders, the six conveners automatically formed the Conveners' Committee—the body through which the major negotiations were conducted with management. The J.S.S.C. could appoint sub-committees, and there were, in fact, three of these. The 'Joint' Production Committee consisted of the Conveners' Committee, and met with management on a regular basis to discuss production schedules. The functions of the two other sub-committees were in fact minimal. The Canteen Committee and Transport Committee—each consisting of two departmental stewards—had very seldom anything to report at the regular monthly meetings of the J.S.S.C. An account of one of the monthly J.S.S.C. meetings is given later.

If there was little competition for the ordinary shop steward's positions, the same could not be said for the position of convener. In the cases of at least two of the unions, the conveners had to contend with strong rivals for the office. The N.U.V.B. convener had held his position for over ten years, but was now subject to sustained pressure and attack from a substantial minority of his stewards—who were supporting the candidacy of an apparently more militant man who had been the leading steward at another factory only three years before. The rival group lobbied individual stewards, and attacks were made in the form of public criticism at J.S.S.C. meetings of their convener's actions. During the period of study there were also two unsuccessful attempts to vote him out of the convenership—attempts which gave rise to pungent private comments from the convener about having to fight battles on three fronts at the same time i.e. against a membership which was generally discontented at short-time working, against the rival for his position, and against a management which was critical of the conveners' faltering control over their members on the shop floor. Then again, the convener of one of the unions with a minority membership at the factory was newly-elected to office, and this victory over his main rival was said to have suprised the other conveners. His position was relatively insecure in that, by union rule, it had to be confirmed every quarter. He was in fact voted out of office during the year following this study, but his initial need to demonstrate militancy and success is given later as one factor in the development of a particular dispute.

Then again, there was certainly rivalry between the conveners for office in the J.S.S.C. itself—a rivalry which was probably encouraged by the full-time officials of the main unions. For example, at a meeting of the N.U.V.B.'s factory committee held at the union offices, the Area Organiser stressed in discussion that the 'standing' of the union required that its convener at the factory be elected to either the chairman's or secretary's office. The point was a live one, because there had just been an election for the chairmanship of the J.S.S.C. following the previous chairman's appointment as Industrial Relations Officer at the factory. At the first meeting of the J.S.S.C. after the appointment, the secretary suggested that standing orders—which required a month's notice of nominations—be dispensed with for the occasion and that the election be conducted forthwith. The T.G.W.U. convener was nominated from the floor—but N.U.V.B. stewards then objected to the procedure. They said that they wanted to nominate their convener for this office, and that they needed time both to persuade him to stand and to canvass on his behalf. A vote was taken on a motion to dispense with standing orders: 27 voted in favour and 25 against the motion. This in turn led to a noisy exchange over the counting of votes. The assistant convener of the T.G.W.U. —a forceful personality—then interrupted the altercation, spoke strongly in favour of the T.G.W.U. convener, and suggested that a special meeting be called within two days to elect a chairman. Time was running short, and this 'compromise' was accepted without a vote or any strong dissension.

On the following day, at a special meeting, the T.G.W.U. convener accepted chairmanship of the J.S.S.C. —there being no other candidate nominated. (The offices of deputy chairman, secretary, and treasurer were held by the conveners of the A.E.U., the N.U.V.B., and the N.S.M.M. respectively.) A number of individual suggestions were given to the author as to why the N.U.V.B. convener declined to stand: on the one hand, that he was concerned to maintain amiable relations within the Convener's Committee, and on the other hand, that he stood no chance of being elected.

He might not have had sufficient support within his own union, and may even have risked losing the secretaryship—from which he would have had to resign in order to accept nomination for the chairmanship. One T.G.W.U. steward suggested that, even had he been assured of all the N.U.V.B. votes, he would not have been successful because some of the A.E.U.'s stewards— said to be unhappy about loss of members to the N.U.V.B. —would have cast their votes in favour of the T.G.W.U. convener. Whatever the reasons might have been, it was clear from the conduct of the earlier meeting that strong union loyalties were functioning at this particular election. Loyalties of this kind were not always the important determinants of who should hold office. For example, the previous chairman had had only a very small union 'party' on the committee, and had held the office for some years because of his obvious abilities. At another car plant, the chairman was similarly the convener of one of the smaller unions. However, in this case, the explanation suggested by some of the conveners concerned was that—in a situation where the larger unions had virtual parity of voting strength and conveners with comparable qualities of leadership—there were many advantages in having an 'impartial' chairman. The hierarchy of workplace labour organization was not without political subtleties.

The diversity of relations between unions and between conveners at the factory level was matched by the diversity of links which the factory labour organisation had with district trade union officials and shop stewards at other factories. These links will be discussed in ascending order of formal recognition or encouragement given by the trade unions. There was no shop steward organisation for the Group—i.e. to cover all the constituent establishments of the firm. However, there was a local Combine Committee, consisting of the conveners of the firm's engine and assembly plants in the area. This Combine Committee was recognised by management, was given facilities for meetings and for inter-factory communication, and was consulted by management on issues which were likely to affect the factories concerned—such as production schedules, for example, or the introduction of a revised pensions scheme. The Combine Committee met monthly to discuss less urgent—or longer-term— problems and policies. For example, the subject matter of one of the regular monthly meetings included the progress made on a demand for higher waiting-time payment, the implications of short-time being worked by a particular gang, transfers of labour between factories, an unexpected restriction of the use of factory telephones by conveners, and the breakdown of communications between the factory Conveners' Committees during a strike which had taken place only a few days before the meeting. Special meetings of the Combine Committee would be convened for matters which could not be held over for a regular meeting, but the pressure of events in some of these matters would often limit communication to telephone conversations.

However, relations between the different Conveners' Committees were often perceptibly strained. A major cause seemed to be resentment on the part of the main engine factory's conveners at what they felt was lack of communications between the factories. They stated that they were not being kept sufficiently informed. The assembly factory's conveners, on the other hand, derided other conveners for having allowed

themselves to be called and used by management as witnesses of a protest march during working hours around an office block by some assembly trackmen. Some of the criticisms were expressed in more personal
terms: members of one committee spoke scornfully of individual members of another, and individual conveners privately deprecated the conduct and assumed motives of members of another committee. Thus the
closest and most regular working relations which the factory's conveners had with other stewards outside the factory during this period were
often stiff-legged and cautious, despite common interests and the encouragement given by the firm to a Combine Committee of this limited
kind.

Regular links between shop stewards at the factory and others in the
district were not maintained on a firm or factory basis. For example,
no one could recall a single occasion when the J.S.S.C. had met with its
counterpart from the factory of any other firm. Not even the usually
small Conveners' Committees of different firms would meet as such
except rarely: the factory's conveners did not know even the names of
many of the conveners at other car factories in the area—except for
those who were members of their own union. There was only one occasion during the period of the study when the conveners sought contact
with those at another firm: the Combine Committee sent a small delegation to one of the Pressed Steel Company's works to check on the validity
of management's claim that a shortage of bodies—and consequential short-
time working in a section of the factory—was due to a dispute at the
Pressed Steel works.

The Confederation of Shipbuilding and Engineering Unions had provision
for linking the J.S.S.C.'s in a district through the accrediting of the chairman and secretaries of each of the committees as 'Confederation Shop
Stewards'. The main purposes of this arrangment are to provide chan-
nels of communication and a system of coordination between unions at
the workplace and the C.S.E.U.'s District Committees. In practice,
the links are tenuous and 'Confederation Stewards' do not think of themselves as such. Although the secretary of this factory's J.S.S.C. did
receive copies of the monthly minutes of the C.S.E.U.'s District Committee—items from which being sometimes discussed at J.S.S.C. meetings—
this was the only form of regular contact or communication. There were
no regular meetings, although the C.S.E.U. would on occasion call special
or ad hoc meetings of all factory conveners in the district. For example,
the firm's Conveners' Committees attended a two-hour meeting(1)
(during working hours) which had been called to discuss the local implementation of an overtime ban which was being applied nationally. But
this kind of meeting between the stewards of different unions at one
work-place and those at another seemed much less frequent than the con-

---

(1) It was interesting that the conveners—despite having intermingled
     before the meeting was opened—seated themselves along firm and
     factory rather than trade union lines. This could, perhaps, be cited
     as an additional indication that—for conveners—factory interests took
     precedence over trade union interests.

tacts arranged by each trade union for its own shop stewards in the district. (1) 1419807

The arrangements made by each of the trade unions for bringing its own shop stewards in the district together from time to time, varied. For example, the T.G.W.U.'s practice seemed to be the most flexible: meetings of conveners or stewards from some or all factories would be called on an ad hoc basis. The N.U.V.B. and the A.E.U. had more systematic arrangements. In the case of the former, there was a Shop Stewards' Council for the district which met monthly and which all of the union's stewards could attend. The A.E.U. had separate meetings each quarter for all conveners in the district, and for all shop stewards. The main business at these regular meetings of the N.U.V.B. and the A.E.U. were the 'factory reports'—which made possible a rough and ready comparison of inter-factory wage rates, earnings, employment positions, steward's facilities, and so on, as well as giving an opportunity to explain particular problems which may have given rise to—or could be the precursors of— repercussions at other factories. The smaller unions at the factory generally had less formalised arrangements for meetings of their shop stewards, but for all the unions—in addition to the special arrangements—there were opportunities for the exchange of views at branch meetings and (for conveners particularly) at the district committee meetings of both the individual unions and those of the C.S.E.U.

One link which the factory had with motor industry shop stewards outside the Midlands was through the N.U.V.B.'s National Shop Stewards' Conference. This body met for a full day at least once a year 'to coordinate the activities of the district shop stewards' committees in furtherence of the aims and policy of the Union'. The factory's assistant convener for the N.U.V.B. was a delegate to this Conference—at which there might sometimes be as many as fifty delegates present. However, the existence of all these links should not be taken to suggest that the factory's shop stewards or conveners formed part of a tightly-knit or very well-informed shop steward network for the district—or even for the car firms in the area. It was possible for the author to attend shop steward meetings of various kinds both during and after the period at the factory. The formation of a network of this kind seemed inhibited by inadequate facilities, poor attendance, and insufficient information. Meetings organised by the individual trade unions —even if they took place frequently— suffered by being confined to members of one union only. Trade union support—and facilities—were generally less readily available for 'mixed-union' organisations. Meetings of shop stewards are often poorly attended. Under these conditions, it is not surprising that the information exchanged tends to be haphazardly selected and of a general or even vague kind. It can be suggested that the problems confronting shop stewards'

_____

(1)   There is a qualification to this statement which is, however, more applicable to other car factories in the area than the one studied. This is that perhaps as many as a third or more of the trade union delegates attending the C.S.E.U. District Committee's monthly meetings were conveners at car factories. The only delegate from the factory studied was the assistant convener of the N.U.V.B.

attempts to form wider networks of relations arise partly from the fact that 'external' relations remain marginal to the main business of shop stewards—whose focus of interest if firmly fixed at shop-floor and factory level.

The most direct link which shop stewards had with their trade unions was, of course, through their relations with full-time officials. The union officials sometimes came to the factory, either singly on a matter pertaining to one union only, or in twos or threes when an issue overlapped union interests. It was seldom that the officials of all the six unions could gather together at one time—to meet either the management or the shop stewards. Several weeks notice was usually required for a meeting of this kind: the conference on the 'state of industrial relations' which was called at only a few day's notice, and which forms the subject of a later section, was a comparative rarity in this respect. An emergency meeting of the factory's shop stewards—called during one of the bigger strikes —could be attended by only four officials—despite the fact that the meeting involved all the unions and was held at 8.00 a.m. on a Monday morning.

Officials were busy men often harried by 'pressures of the moment'. They were rarely observed at the factory, and almost never on the shop floor. Most factory workers probably saw their union officials only at strike meetings—at which it was more than likely that they were being exhorted by the officials to return to work. Under these conditions, the heavy work-load under which most full-time officials laboured were sometimes not appreciated. Some N.U.V.B. members, for example, said that their officials could not be seen to do them any good, and that they resented the payment of dues—which they considered too high for what they received in return. At this time there were many cases of N.U.V.B. members who were seriously in arrears with their union contributions. Special card checks were organised, and a strong and specifically-worded threat was posted on the union notice boards at the factory to the effect that fines would have to be imposed if the arrears were not reduced. To the worker, his shop steward was the union, and his interest in union affairs was larely confined to workplace problems.

By comparison with some other car factories, the facilities provided by the management for conveners and the J.S.S.C. were reasonable—even generous. The Conveners' Committee was explicitly recognised as a negotiating body, and was in practice consulted on a wide range of issues. Conveners could raise almost any matter they wished with senior management—and receive a hearing. For departmental stewards, there was a regular meeting of the J.S.S.C. for an hour or two each month, held on the premises during working hours. While permission for irregular or special meetings of shop stewards had to be obtained from the management in each case, this permission was not often refused (although there was a move by management to reduce the number of meetings during the later stages of the study). Meetings of the J.S.S.C. were held in a conference room in the Personnel Department—and then later in a canteen (after structural alterations to accommodate the new Industrial Relations Officer had absorbed the conference room). While departmental stewards had to obtain specific permission from their supervisors to leave their departments or consult with other stewards, the conveners could move about the factory at will (a freedom on which restrictions were also later imposed). Conveners were entitled to use any factory telephone for internal calls or to call their union offices.

The conveners did not have the use of an office. The secretary of the J.S.S.C. had been given a locker for records and equipment, to be kept at his 'normal' place of work (which was with a rectification gang near the final line)—but this was later moved, by agreement, to a more convenient site in a machinery room in the paint shop. The Industrial Relations Officer's secretary (who had been secretary to the Personnel Manager before the Industrial Relations Officer's appointment) was permitted to undertake typing given to her by the secretary of the J.S.S.C. The Conveners' Committee met regularly and formally each week in a canteen. No minutes of these meetings were kept. For the rest of the week, there were customary places where each convener was likely to be found. For example, 'Ernie's shelter'—a small paint shop boilerhouse where a labourer kept his gear (and provided tea)—was the place to enquire the whereabouts of the T.G.W.U. convener. The N.U.V.B. convener was often to be found in a 'rest room' in one of the trim shops, while the S.M.W.U. convener seemed more elusive, but was fairly frequently to be found in a clerk's office in the body shop. The other conveners were often at their workplaces.

The conveners—like all stewards—had to 'clock on' punctually: there were no privileges in this regard. Because the conveners had no office, communications from management travelled by a number of routes and media. Telephone calls would be made to prospective places where conveners might be found—and supervisors might, in addition, act as 'runners'. 'Ernie's shelter' was some distance from a telephone, but within range of the factory's public address system—which was used to call the conveners together when there was an emergency. There were some areas in the factory which were out of convenient range of a telephone, and out of range of the 'Tannoy': it was occasionally tactically or personally convenient for a convener to be 'unavailable' when called—either by management or by stewards of their own union. Conveners led very busy working lives, and like managers, had sometimes to be 'in conference' to avoid giving offence by making priorities explicit.

Most shop stewards spent most of their working time at their regular jobs. It is difficult to generalise about the amount of working time spent on 'Union business' because of the wide variations between individual stewards, departmental requirements, and periods of normality and 'crisis'. An average of between five and ten hours each week would not have been too far out, perhaps, during the period of this study. Three of the conveners were in fact full-time negotiators and 'troubleshooters', while the other three seemed to spend on average about ten to fifteen hours a week on union business. This 'union business' was, of course, conducted almost entirely within the factory and it was only very occasionally that a departmental steward would have to leave the factory during working hours. Conveners might do so once or twice a month— and then seldom for more than an hour or two. Examples of this 'union business' outside the factory were some of the meetings of the Combine

Committee, the meeting of conveners called by the C.S.E.U. (referred to above), the delegation to the Pressed Steel Company's works (also referred to above), and a visit by the N.U.V.B. convener to his union office to discuss with his official a drift of his members out of the factory to other car firms.

Shop stewards on union business during working hours could be paid from several sources. For attendance at the regular monthly J.S.S.C. meetings, departmental stewards would be paid by the firm. But this payment was only at the 'basic' hourly wage rate and omitted the bonus supplements. Stewards earning piece-work rates said that they would thus receive about half their normal hourly earnings for this time. The difference between basic and average earnings was in fact made up by claims from a Shop Stewards' Fund (at the beginning of the period) and from individual trade union resources, or sometimes from a departmental fund (at the end of the period—the Shop Stewards' Fund having in fact been bankrupted meanwhile). But in all three cases it was the workers who were making up the pay of their stewards. The case of stewards paid at time rates was similar: the firm paid only basic hourly rates, and the balance or bonus element was refunded by a straightforward claim against the Shop Stewards' Fund of seven shillings and sixpence for each J.S.S.C. meeting. All departmental stewards could also claim against the fund, or, later, against their special ad hoc union or departmental funds, for other 'loss of earnings' during the time spent on trade union matters.

The financial compensation of conveners was more complicated. It was the usual practice for the full-time negotiators to 'book' a few hours each week as having been spent at their 'normal' jobs. This was a mutually acceptable arrangement, as supervisors had to countersign the 'time sheet' or claim, and some 'middle' management certainly knew of the practice. Payment for these few hours was calculated at the average hourly piece work earnings of the workers or gang with whom the convener would have worked (or did in fact work in the case of conveners of the smaller unions). The remaining hours of the standard working week would be claimed as time spent on negotiation. Because workers' contributions to the Shop Stewards' Fund were deducted from wages, the firm did not pay for all the hours claimed as time spent on negotiation, but made an adjustment. The 'negotiating' hours spent by all conveners each week were totalled and converted to a sum of wages in the same way as for those hours claimed as having been actually worked. From this sum was then deducted the total contributions to the Shop Stewards' Fund for that week (and a sum representing an adjustment for tax purposes). The fund was never sufficient to meet the conveners' 'wages' for conveners' negotiating time, and there was thus always a balance —which was made up by the firm as an 'ex-gratia payment' and distributed between the conveners in proportion to the hours booked and subject to normal P.A.Y.E. deductions. In short, the conveners were paid the average of what other men in their sections earned, and the firm set off the workers' contributions to the Shop Stewards' Fund against this cost. This arrangement seemed to be at least partially due to the belief amongst both stewards and management that the Shop Stewards' Fund had been abused in the past (although it was not possible to obtain a convincing account of the technique of the alleged abuse).

The Shop Stewards' Fund was for this factory only, and was derived from two main sources. At the time of engagement, all hourly-paid employees were invited by the Employment Officer to contribute—by weekly deductions from wages—to the firm's Benevolent Fund, its Sports and Social Club, a number of charities, an independent hospital and sick benefit fund, and the Shop Stewards' Fund. The Employment Officer said that in practice nearly everybody agreed to all these deductions. Contributions to the Shop Stewards' Fund were one penny a week for day-workers, women and youths, and twopence a week for trackmen and piece-workers. Shortly, before the field-work for this study began, the J.S.S.C. had resolved that the rate of contributions to the fund be doubled. Management had no objections, and stewards undertook to have each worker sign an agreement accordingly. But the increased deductions were delayed for some months: not only were individual shop stewards opposed to the move on the grounds that the increased contributions were merely saving the firm money, but many workers were themselves against increased deductions at a time when there were many weeks of short-time working. Suspicions were also voiced about the uses to which the Fund was put, and stewards demanded—and obtained—first quarterly, then monthly, accounts from the treasurer of the J.S.S.C. One of these statements is reproduced in Section F and gives an impression of the sums involved. (1)

Secondly, the fund included the proceeds of a 'tote'--run by and for the factory employees only. The promoters were the Conveners' Committee and the firm took no part in its administration. The system was simple: for sixpence a choice, any two numbers between 0 and 40 could be selected. These were marked on printed tote tickets, and stewards were the collectors (some supervisors also acted as collectors). Rewards for collection were the free selection of numbers at the end of each completed ticket. Administration was reduced by having 'permanents', i.e. tickets retained by the J.S.S.C. treasurer from week to week, the selected numbers remaining unchanged. Of the total weekly takings, one-eighth was retained for the shop stewards' Fund, and seven-eights was distributed as prize money. The total takings tended to decline during the period of the study, until special efforts were made to improve administration.

The draw took place each week, in the canteen, and after working hours. The determination of winning entries seldom took less than an hour, and there were very few persons who were enthusiastic enough to watch the draw through to the end. The 'draw' consisted of two numbered balls being withdrawn at random from a bag containing 42 balls—this was the winning combination. The 42nd ball was a white one—the 'snowball', for which there was a separate draw. If the white ball was drawn, then an accumulated 'jackpot' would go to that week's winning numbers in addition to what they had already won.

_____

(1) Trade union finance includes more elements than are contained in the accounts presented annually by the Registrar of Friendly Societies. Contributions to, and costs of, workplace organisation seem to be largely omitted from the Registrar's Reports.

An example may be given: for one week the total takings were just over £160, and there were 24 winners. Each received £5.14s. and a sum of £5 went into the 'jackpot'. There were hazards in the system, for, on this occasion, it was later discovered that there had been 25 entries of the winning combination: the extra man was paid out and the loss was absorbed from the fund.(1) Winning numbers were usually chalked up on a notice board in the canteen, and were invariably spread about by word of mouth.

Although virtually all of the hourly-paid workers at the factory were trade union members, the labour organisation was structurally untidy and administratively amateurish—in strong contrast to one popular view that shop stewards' organisations are powerful and often autocratic. The untidiness seemed less important than might have been expected: while the Conveners' Committee and the J.S.S.C. could act independently of the trade unions' district machinery, shop-floor influence on the stewards' policies and activities was strong—if not overwhelming. Despite the sometimes casual arrangements for the election of stewards, there was no absence of 'workshop democracy'. Neither workers nor stewards felt multi-unionism to be a problem in itself; it did not form the subject-matter of disputes, although it could complicate the settlement of disputes about other issues (as will be shown in later sections). The resources of the factory's labour organisation could be seen largely in terms of the abilities of its leadership, the recognition and goodwill it received from management, the quality of the information on which its decisions were based, and the adequacy of its financial means. Workers acknowledged the importance of general competence—both of their own representatives and of management. This acknowledgement, together with competition for the convenerships, ensured a sufficient and often a high standard of competence amongst the leadership. On the other hand, the conveners were vulnerable because they had to rely not only on the continuing support of their members but on managerial goodwill as well (over the matter of facilities and consultation, for example), because of the generally unsystematic receipt of information from management and union sources outside the factory, and because of inadequate finance.

---

(1) There were occasional contributions to be set off against such hazards. For example, over the years correspondence had developed between the managing director of one of the firm's distributors and the secretary of the J.S.S.C. Letters were received by the secretary during some of the larger strikes, pointing out the 'loss' of production and requesting that the conveners 'stick to procedure' and prevent strikes. However, at Christmas there was often a contribution of £20-£25 to the stewards 'merriment fund'.

E   Industrial Relations Machinery: Procedures

This section provides a brief outline of the factory's formal and informal procedures for avoiding or handling disputes or disagreements between management and workpeople. As a member of the Engineering Employers' Federation, the firm formally operated the procedures specified in the engineering 'Procedure—Manual Workers' agreement of 1922 (as amended in 1955).(1) In its essentials, this agreement provides that matters in dispute ('questions arising') shall—when remaining unsettled—be referred by the aggrieved party through a succession of stages or meetings before any strike action is taken. The agreement specifies the number of stages, but does not give much detail about their composition or mode of operation. However, a distinction may be made between those stages that may normally be expected to take place at the workplace—or 'domestically'— and those which are held away from the factory—sometimes called 'formal' or 'official' procedure.

Workers are required to raise any grievance or question arising first with their foreman; their shop steward—if they have one—is given no function at this stage. Failing a settlement (and assuming the existence of a steward) the steward and one of the workmen concerned may take the issue to the 'head shop-foreman' or shop manager. If there is still no agreement, the matter may be taken either to a 'Works Committee' as set up under the procedure agreement (very few of these Works Committees have been formed) or to a Works Conference. Works Conferences appear in the agreement as 'deputations of workmen who may be accompanied by their Organiser (in which event a representative of the Employers' Association shall also be present)'. The agreement does not provide a place for conveners or senior stewards as such, nor does it specify how many persons are entitled to attend at each stage in the series of meetings. Trade union officials and representatives of the employers' association are almost invariably in attendance at Works Conferences. Works Conferences may thus be regarded alternately as the final stage in 'domestic' procedure, or as the first stage of 'official' procedure.

Continued failure to agree takes the issue to a Local Conference held away from the factory, and where—in practice—a panel of employers drawn from federated firms not directly involved in the dispute hears the case presented by union officials and managers of the firm (assisted by officials of the employers' association). Issues which are then still

---

(1) On the general development, principles and practice of engineering 'Procedure', see Arthur Marsh, Industrial Relations in Engineering (Oxford: Pergamon, 1965), chaps. IV and V.

unresolved may be referred to a meeting of union and employers' 'national' representatives, which is held monthly at York in the form of a number of 'courts', and is called 'Central Conference'. The procedure allows Central Conference to 'make a joint recommendation to the constituent bodies.' If not settled, the issue may be held over for further information, or be referred back for works or local discussion or settlement. It is not until these 'references back' have been followed through, or until Central Conference is 'unable to arrive at a mutual recommendation', that a strike over the dispute is constitutional. There is no provision for arbitration at any stage of procedure, nor for standing joint committees or decision-making bodies of trade unions and employers to settle their differences. In most disputes, workers are required to continue to work on management's terms until the matter is settled or procedure is exhausted.

The remainder of this section is concerned with 'domestic' procedures only.(1) It is well known that formal domestic procedure—as laid down in the engineering agreement—has been supplemented and modified at different workplaces, in different ways, and with greater or lesser degrees of formality. Indeed, one of the amendments introduced in 1955 into the agreement suggested that procedure could be improved by consultation, particularly 'in the initial avoidance of disputes'. Modifications of the domestic procedure in the factory studied seem to have been made fairly frequently over the past few years. Amongst the general reasons which might be suggested for these changes are the expansion of the firm and factory—which would make more formal, bureaucratic (and less autocratic) procedures a logical development; the limitations which 'personality conflicts' amongst the key individuals inevitably impose on the operation of formal arrangements; and—not least—the fact that continued labour unrest would itself suggest that improved procedures might be desirable.

For example, before 1957, there seems to have been little managerial delegation of authority to settle disputes at shop-floor level. A circular issued by the management in this year referred to difficulties which had arisen because 'Supervision' had previously had no authority to settle labour problems within their own departments. It was stated that a new policy being put into effect '...will vest increasing responsibility in all grades of Supervision. They will in future be fully authorised to conduct all Shop-floor negotiations with the Shop Stewards concerned, i.e. Shop Steward with Chargehand, Chargehand with Foreman'.(2) Only in cases where 'difficulty' was encountered was a shop matter to be taken to higher authority—i.e. to the Superintendent together with the Works

---

(1) The factory was not directly involved in Local or Central Conferences during the period of this study, and the observer was not able to attend any formal Works Conferences. However, a 'quasi-Works Conference' is discussed in a later section of this paper.

(2) Chargehands were later called 'junior foremen'. The main reason for this change was said to be the absence of any reference to 'chargehands' in engineering 'Procedure'.

Manager or Production Manager. The circular continued: '...this procedure will enable the Shop Stewards to settle matters arising within their own Departments, thus avoiding complicated conferences on matters which are the immediate concern of the Department, and eliminate the necessity for a weekly Shop Stewards' Meeting where it is felt that there has been much difficulty in dealing with problems which are better resolved at Shop-Floor level, and also avoid the by-passing of Shop Supervision which has possibly been the cause of much friction in the past.'

By 1960, the 'Negotiating Procedure'—as it appeared on paper—seemed to have become more like that in operation at the time of the study. It formally recognised a shop steward hierarchy, and regulated the intervention of the Convener's Committee. Workers first raised a matter with their foreman; the steward was then brought in to assist; and at the third step, the case was taken by the steward to the superintendent. If—after this third stage—a steward got no satisfaction, then he could call in his convener. It was laid down that 'where there are more than one union involved it has been agreed that for the purpose of smoother working the convener of the union of which the Shop Steward concerned is a member will be able to conduct the case up to the level of Executive, where the shop steward or the management can call in the rest of the Conveners' Committee'. The Conveners stressed at that time—as also verbally during the study— that issues should wherever possible be settled at shop floor level: there would thus be a minimum of delay, and some easing of the work-load of conveners themselves.

Two months before the appointment of the Industrial Relations Officer the 'procedure to be observed in industrial relations' was stipulated by the Group Director in a memorandum to senior and middle management. This procedure was to apply to both staff and manual workers. The initial step by the aggrieved worker was now to be to his 'immediate' supervisor—i.e. the junior foreman. Steward and foreman entered at the second stage. Failing agreement, the steward was obliged to bring in his convener, and the foreman was obliged to refer the matter to the superintendent or departmental head. The fourth stage was to consist of the Personnel Executive, the production executive concerned, and 'if necessary' the union official. In other words, union officials now had authority from management to enter procedure before Works Conference stage—and this latter was not held to be part of 'domestic procedure' at all. At the fifth stage in this domestic procedure, the matter could be referred to the Personnel Executive and the manager concerned, and these negotiations would be 'referred' to the Works Manager 'whose word will be final in regard to all matters concerning industrial relations'. Not withstanding this, the sixth—or Works Conference—stage specified that the Works Manager, Personnel and departmental Executives and the appropriate superintendent be present, together with 'stewards' and union officials ('as they decide').

This was a considerable 'escalation' of stages, and was to be an unstable situation both because of the new position of Industrial Relations Officer, and because the conveners did not accept the first stage—and hastened to remove the junior foremen from the procedure 'by negotiation' and by—probably deliberate—neglect. Thus, a man might take an individual grievance to his junior foreman, but would be more likely to consult his steward first—when both he and his steward would see the foreman as the first step. For some weeks after his appointment, the formal role of the Industrial Relations Officer in procedure was not specified. It was then clarified: he was to enter procedure at the executive level, taking over from the Personnel Executive most of the negotiations with hourly-paid workers. In practice, because of the novelty of his appointment, the close links he retained with his former colleagues (who accepted his change of sides with good grace if not without inevitable and increasing reservation), and because he was in practice absorbing the status and functions of his immediate superior—i.e. the Personnel Executive—the Industrial Relations Officer had in fact soon participated at almost all levels in the procedures. An example of such interventions are related in the section on a 'breach of procedure' strike. The conveners put the matter succinctly in their half-jocular references to him as a 'one-man band'.

Illustration II opposite gives a brief outline of the formal procedural stages for the settlement of disputes at the factory which seemed to be in effect for most of the period of the study. 'Seemed to be' because of misunderstandings or disagreements over what formal procedure was supposed to be on some occasions, because of explicit flexibility as to which stage it might be agreed to put matters 'into procedure', and because—in any event—formal procedure could hardly operate without a heavy overlay of informal consultation and discussion. An example of a disagreement about the constitution of a stage in procedure, and of flexibility in the use of procedure, both occur in the 'breach of procedure' strike given in detail later in the paper. Here, it is sufficient to note that—in relation to a meeting at the superintendent stage of procedure—management argued the right to have in attendance at the meeting members of their own choice (irrespective of the formal role these persons might have at later stages), and accepted that the union had the same right.

A number of points about the domestic procedure at the factory may be briefly mentioned. Firstly, over the few years preceding the study at least, there had been change and experimentation—and particularly an attempt to ensure the solution of problems at the shop-floor level wherever this was possible. Secondly, both management and the conveners stated that issues should, if possible, be kept within the factory. Management justified the number of stages on these grounds. The conveners, for their part, were not wont to complain about the number of stages as such, but were more critical of delays in the operation of procedure. Criticism of the number of stages seemed to be incidental to the question of delay. Thirdly, informal procedures—or what might be called prior consultation—mostly took precedence over procedure. They were in operation all the time: there was an ongoing and mutual exchange of information, testing of feelings, and subtle requesting of advice. A 'hot-line' was always open between management and conveners. There was no formal institution of 'joint consultation' (as opposed to negotiation)—nor did this seem to be required. Ad hoc 'consultation' would take place occasionally—as when the Industrial Relations Officer called a meeting

44

Illustration II

'DOMESTIC' DISPUTES PROCEDURE: FORMAL STAGES AND
PROBABLE ATTENDANCE

Union official/s Convener/s (Departmental steward)	Stage 5 WORKS CONFERENCE	Association officials Works Manager Personnel Executive Industrial Relations Officer
(Official) Convener/s (Steward)	Stage 4 PERSONNEL EXECUTIVE	(Works Manager) Personnel Executive Executive Industrial Relations Officer
Convener/s Steward/s	Stage 3 INDUSTRIAL RELATIONS OFFICER	Executive Industrial Relations Officer Superintendent
Convener Steward (Worker)	Stage 2 SUPERINTENDENT	Superintendent Foreman (Junior foreman)
Steward Workers	Stage 1 FOREMAN	Foreman Junior foreman

Notes

(1) Brackets denote persons present on only some occasions.

(2) The diagram makes allowance for single and joint union references.

(3) The firm and the conveners drew a distinction between 'domestic procedure'—which ended with Stage 4—and 'official procedure'—which began with Stage 5, probably because Works Conferences were usually held at the offices of the employers' association.

of the Combine Committee to give details of a revised pension scheme the firm was putting into effect. It was usually only when the informal process was no longer sufficient that issues were formally 'put into procedure'.

Finally, whereas in theory an agreement cannot be held to be functioning while one party is in default, and while management would sometimes firmly 'refuse to negotiate' while an unconstitutional strike was taking place, in practice the informal procedures would often be conducted mc expeditiously and with a greater sense of urgency at such times. It must be a rare occurrence for informal negotiations, with the purpose 'finding a formula for a return to work to allow negotiations to take place', to be conducted without reference to the substantive matters in dispute (although, again, the final stages in the 'breach of procedure' strike recounted later must have come close to this).

PART II

Joint Shop Stewards' Committee Meetings

In some respects, the factory's labour organisation could be compared with that of a (British) political party: departmental stewards were the elected M.P.'s of a workshop government in opposition; parliamentary activity was conducted at the ordinary and special meetings of the J.S.S.C.; and the Conveners' Committee was a small 'shadow cabinet' whose leader could influence but not determine the appointment of his colleagues. The political analogy holds good to the extent that the trade unions did not in practice provide a higher or governing body to control the J.S.S.C., and is invalid to the extent that there was no workshop equivalent of a professional civil service. The analogy may serve to highlight the functions and conduct of the J.S.S.C. meetings. The functions were to discuss and determine general policy (the conveners would some- times say that they themselves as a committee did not make policy), to co-ordinate the viewpoints and activities of workshop and trade union 'constituencies', and to provide a clearing house for information rele- vant to the functioning of the 'party' as well as for dissemination amongst the electorate. The rules and procedures for the conduct of ordinary meetings of the J.S.S.C. were determined by its constitution (or 'standing orders' which the firm in practice recognised), by agreements with management, and by 'custom and practice'.

Ordinary—or regular—meetings of the J.S.S.C. were held during the last hour or two of the dayshift on the first Wednesday of each month. Re- minders were often telephoned to each department by the Industrial Re- lations Officer's secretary a few hours before the meetings were due to take place. Stewards who worked on nightshift could, of course, attend the meetings in their own time. However, there was rather little shift- working at the factory at the time of the study, very few such stewards, and these latter were not observed to attend any of the J.S.S.C. meetings. The meetings had been held first in a conference room in the Personnel Department, but structural alterations made it necessary to change the venue to a canteen building. The conference room had been small and stuffy; the canteen was too large, and very noisy because of the clearing- up activity of the kitchen staff.

Attendance at the meetings varied each month, but there were usually about sixty stewards present. Of those who were not present, some were absent on the day, a few were on nightshift, some were sorting out departmental difficulties, some had forgotten that there was to be a meeting, and one or two may not have bothered to attend. Stewards would leave their departments five minutes or so before the meetings were due to start; and they could—and were prepared—to leave the factory immediately after the meetings. Starting times were fairly elastic: the meetings were usually called to order ten to fifteen minutes after the time laid down. This made allowance for latecomers, and permitted the exchange of information and lobbying activities between stewards, some of whom would not otherwise normally meet each other. Meetings never ended before the dayshift finished, and seldom continued for very long thereafter.

The following is a brief account of one of these half-dozen regular J.S.S.C. meetings which took place during the period of the study. An examination of minute books, and attendance at other meetings, indicate that in most respects the meeting was not untypical. There was a more or less customary order of business at J.S.S.C. meetings (minutes, correspondence, production report, conveners' reports, other business, treasurer's report, canteen and transport committee reports), but the order was sometimes deliberately or unwittingly altered to take account of the urgency and interest of particular items—as happened at this meeting. The chairman opened the proceedings by acknowledging that a number of important issues had arisen since the previous monthly meeting, although he said that he thought it would be preferable to adhere to the customary order of business.

The minutes of the previous meeting were brief, and after being read out by the secretary, they were accepted as a true record. There were no queries about the minutes on most occasions, nor—on this occasion— was there any discussion arising out of items in the minutes. It was customary to follow the reading of the minutes with the reading out and discussion of items selected by the secretary from the minutes of the previous month's meeting of the C.S.E.U. District Committee. In this instance, it was noted that the annual holidays for the following year would probably be taken during the same weeks as had become customary, but that various difficulties were to be the subject of a meeting between the C.S.E.U. and the local employers' association.

The chairman of the Joint Production Committee (who was the deputy-chairman of the J.S.S.C.) then gave the production report. This was usually a major item on the agenda as questions of production delays and short-time or overtime working arose out of the report. The numbers of cars of each model which had been produced during the previous working week were read out—and many stewards made a note of the figures. The management had only recently instituted a weekly meeting of the Joint Production Committee in order that production schedules could be reviewed for a week ahead. It could now thus be stated that a full or normal week would be worked during the current week unless there was a major breakdown or a strike, but that there could be a recurrence of short-time working during the following week unless a dispute in the bodyshop was quickly settled—and unless the bodyshop workers also agreed to then work overtime. Because the stock of bodies to be sent along the tracks was very low, the conveners had advised the

48

bodyshop gang to agree to work overtime, but this had been refused pending settlement of the dispute. The issue was opened to discussion and a track steward bluntly asked whether the dispute did not result mainly from 'personality conflict and enmity' between the S.M.W.U. convener and an N.U.V.B. steward in the bodyshop. Neither steward was then present at the meeting (the S.M.W.U. convener arrived later) and the discussion veered to the role of the Conveners' Committee in disputes which may only technically be said to concern a single union.

After a strike by sheet metal workers a month before—which had put members of other unions out of work—it had been noted by many stewards that the Conveners' Committee had not acted formally until the final stages of the dispute. At a special meeting of stewards, a proposal had been made that it be obligatory for the Conveners' Committee to be called in by the relevant convener under such circumstances. A supporter of this proposal—who was a S.M.W.U. steward—had now written to the J.S.S.C. secretary to formally withdraw his support of the proposal. His reason was given as 'the town policy of his union'—and the letter was read out to the meeting. The man was not present, the meaning of 'town policy' was not apparent, and the letter caused surprise and some muttering. There the matter had to rest for the time being, and the production report was then concluded. Management believed that new tracks for a new model could become operative within a fortnight, although there would as yet be only a small number of the cars produced. Transfers of men to the new tracks had already been taking place, and, following a suggestion from the floor, it was agreed that management be asked to use existing labour in the factory on the new model (although there was already an agreement in effect that no new labour would be engaged during periods when there was short-time working).

Two matters more appropriately classifiable as 'other business' then arose. Firstly, a written report on a proposed revision of the J.S.S.C.'s standing orders had been promised at the previous meeting—but had not been circulated yet. The secretary reported that a new constitution was still under review, and that it would probably be based on that adopted by the engine factory's J.S.S.C. The other matter was a request for information: the secretary had previously obtained information from the local employment exchange about the procedure whereby men who had been laid-off work could claim unemployment pay. What was the position of those men living outside the coverage of the local employment exchange? The secretary undertook to find out, and report back.

The next item was correspondence. A letter had been received from the strike committee of a firm asking for support. The stewards agreed to undertake departmental collections in aid of the strike. The chairman then expressed some concern: at the previous monthly meeting the J.S.S.C. had had a similar appeal from men on strike at a local engineering firm, and the stewards had undertaken to make a collection. The response had been poor, having produced a total sum of about £15 only. The chairman said it was clear that there were stewards who had not in fact made a collection. He redressed them, and appealed for a better response this time, saying that such small sums would only serve to make the committee appear foolish to others. There were two further letters (one of which—from the S.M.W.U. steward—had already been dealt with). The other was from the strike committee of yet another firm asking the conveners to meet a deputation. This was agreed.

The 'conveners' reports' then followed: information was given rapidly by each convener in turn. It was not possible for the observer to note them all—nor did they all appear in the minutes of the meeting. But the main ones may be briefly listed. The N.U.V.B. convener spoke of the difficulty he was having in getting management to agree to recognise two additional stewards on particular tracks, and referred to a previous affair when a steward had been suspended, to suggest that there was a managerial tightening up on stewards' facilities. Another problem confronting him concerned the manning of one of the tracks. But the most important matter from his point of view—and he said that it was a matter for all unions—was to make progress on a previous decision of the committee to demand higher waiting-time payments. His Area Organiser had made enquiries about the rates paid in other car factories in the district: he had the letter and read out the different rates. It seemed that they were all higher than the rate being paid by the firm. When questioned, he admitted that progress on the issue was taking time—he had himself received the letter from his official two months before. However, the Combine Committee would now be taking the matter further at a meeting to be held on the following day.

The A.E.U. convener then reported. He had only one main point, and this was contained in a letter which one of his stewards had received from the firm's Work Study Executive. The letter stated that the piece-work prices on an existing model which was being transferred to the new tracks would be cancelled, and that new prices would be fixed. This information raised a number of comments from the floor that trouble could be expected, but it also raised a question of procedure. Why—it was asked from the floor—was the letter received by the steward and not by the convener? It was held that this was the kind of practice that was undermining the J.S.S.C. The question implied that the matter was one which would affect other unions in the same department, and should have been dealt with by the conveners. The convener's reply was that he usually received copies of letters of this kind, but that somebody must have 'slipped up' in this instance. The chairman interjected that he did not think it was an issue worth pursuing, that it was just an omission, and this was accepted.

The A.S.W.M. convener had nothing to report, and the N.S.M.M. convener had only one item: he was concerned that the firm had 'put out' some brasswork to a non-union firm while there was short time working in his own department—where the items could be manufactured. He was pursuing the matter. The S.M.W.U. convener had arrived at the meeting late, seemed to have been informed by his colleagues about the earlier discussion of his union's 'town policy', and took the opportunity to explain that the decision of the steward who had previously commented on this to withdraw his support of the proposal that the Conveners' Committee be brought immediately into any issues likely to affect more than one union, was a personal one. The 'town policy' referred to the protection of union autonomy, but was not an inflexible one. He said that the letter was really only a 'hangover' from a previous dispute, and that he had nothing further to report.

The chairman (T.G.W.U.) reported on an issue of redundancy in the paint shop. Management had apparently given a categorical assurance that a change of method in the paint shop would not lead to any redundancy: any temporary over-manning would be met by short-time working. Nineteen men were now being moved out of the paint shop. However this was only a technical redundancy, as they were being transferred to other jobs. There was to be a meeting with management about this issue on the following morning, and the convener assured the stewards that no one would be allowed to be declared redundant. He then reported on the progress which had been made on the negotiation of separate bonus schemes for groups of day-workers, such as storemen and inspectors. Management had proposed that the efficiency of the latter would be examined, but that only about 5 per cent of the inspectors was likely to be affected. In any event it was hoped that a separate meeting of day-workers' stewards could soon be arranged to discuss these matters.

The treasurer then presented the monthly income and expenditure report of the J.S.S.C. The monthly figures were not typical—as the period had involved part of the annual holiday—but it was pointed out that the financial situation was becoming critical and that something would soon have to be done to raise funds. What was seen as the failure of an attempt to increase contributions to the Shop Stewards' Fund was referred to. The treasurer pointed out also that there had been some reluctance on the part of the auditors (two departmental stewards elected by the J.S.S.C.) to sign the accounts owing to heavy claims from some sections. He gave no further details and the statement raised no comment. The quarterly Balance Sheet (reproduced as Illustration III overleaf) was then distributed and discussed. There was one copy for each steward: the chairman stated that stewards could show them to any member who asked, but not to let the copies leave their possession. (1) It was moved that the treasurer's report be accepted, and this was agreed.

There were now only twenty minutes or so to the end of the working day and the chairman said that there had been a request from the Industrial Relations Officer to address the meeting. The Conveners' Committee had given permission, and hoped that this would be acceptable to the J.S.S.C. The Industrial Relations Officer then entered, and made two brief points. The first was that there had been some justified criticism in the past about delays on the part of the management over the handling of issues in dispute. He said that he himself regarded this as an important matter, had taken steps to speed things up over the past months and would continue to do so. The other point was to make known his willingness to 'come along to meet the stewards at any time on any issue to explain the firm's policies'. He said he was willing to answer any questions there and then.

---

(1) The coveners have been asked whether the balance sheet could be reproduced, and have made no objection.

Illustration III

QUARTERLY BALANCE SHEET OF SHOP STEWARDS' FUND
QUARTER ENDING 30TH JUNE

	£	s	d
Balance in bank on 31st March	147.	18.	6
Cash in Hand on 31st March	12.	5.	6
	160.	4.	0

Income

	£	s	d
Contributions deducted from wages	278.	13.	10
Net proceeds from stewards' tote	127.	2.	6
Accumulated 'Snowball' (or Jackpot)	26.	0.	0
Interest		9.	6
	592.	9.	10

Expenditure

	£	s	d
Claims from stewards	449.	11.	10
Wreath (death of union official)	2.	2.	0
Printed tote tickets	2.	15.	6
Presentation (to an ex-convener at the factory, now a full-time official of his union)	10.	10.	0
Bank Charge		2.	0
	464.	11.	4
Cash at bank on 30th June	127.	18.	6
	592.	9.	10

Note: the Quarter does not include any part of the annual holiday period.

The first response came from the floor: the Industrial Relations Officer had said nothing, and why had he really come? In reply, the two points were repeated. Another steward raised an instance of delays: an issue had arisen on his track a week before, and had been reported to the Conveners' Committee on three occasions. He said that his convener had requested a meeting with the Tracks Executive, but without success. It was felt that although the matter was now 'dead' it might have brought the works to a halt at the time. The Industrial Relations Officer replied that the case had not come to his notice. The matter rested there, no one raised further queries, and the manager left the meeting.

The attendance of managers was very untypical of shop stewards' meetings. In the few remaining minutes of the meeting, it seemed to be agreed —in response to a suggestion from a deputy-convener—that the only reason the Industrial Relations Officer had come to the meeting was to get permission to put the firm's point of view to the stewards, or, as he put it, 'to crash stewards' meetings'. Management had tried to do this in the past, and had been prevented from doing so. The chairman assured the meeting that existing policy in this regard would continue to apply: that if management wanted to meet the shop stewards, then management could call special meetings for the purpose. (Although the Industrial Relations Officer subsequently made many requests for permission to attend and address the meetings, these were refused.) By this time, the stream of workers out of the factory was flowing strongly, stewards were slipping out of the door, and the meeting was breaking up in an end-of-term atmosphere. Somebody moved 'standing orders', and the room was cleared very quickly. In this respect, the meeting was quite characteristic.

The factory's shop stewards met together formally on other occasions. There were full meetings of the J.S.S.C. for special purposes: the chairman and secretary—acting together—had the power to call these meetings (although, as has been mentioned, if they were to be held in working time and on the factory premises, management's prior permission was required). The chairman and secretary could also call for partial or sectional stewards' meetings. For example, there were meetings of 'track stewards', and of 'day-workers' stewards'. The number of such full or partial ad hoc meetings was very variable: there might be three or four in one week, although on average about one a week was held during the period of study. No minutes were kept for any of these special meetings.

Finally, a few remarks may be made about the general conduct of the shop stewards' meetings which were attended by the observer during the period of study. Control from the chair—although weakened under the stress of events to be recounted in the following sections—was usually flexible but nevertheless firm, and conventional rules of procedure and debate were generally observed. Discussions were often heated, but were seldom acrimonious. Personal animosities—known to be present— did not often show themselves publicly. The discussion was never patently 'ideological'(1) but was of a very practical kind: a casual observer would have been hard put to it sometimes to find the generality in a mass of detail and factory jargon. The occasional impractical suggestion—for example, that the Minister of Labour be asked to hold an inquiry into 'mismanagement' at the factory—was lightly derided from the floor, and easily side-stepped by the chairman. As might be expected, some stewards had more to say on all matters than others. 'They just loved to rattle', as one convener put it. Others were not observed to speak at all (in some cases, this disposition being reflected in the absence of any 'report back' meetings at departmental level). The way in which the cohesion and administration of the J.S.S.C. became less effective under difficult circumstances and sustained pressures from both management and the shop floor workers, served to emphasise the important part the J.S.S.C. had in the maintenance of a strong and coherent trade union organisation at the workplace—whatever reservations might be made about the purposes to which such an organisation might be put.

(1) It is appropriate to note here that only one shop steward at the factory was known to be a member of the Communist Party. He was a relatively young man, and did not speak often at J.S.S.C. meetings. What he did say was not notably militant. In private discussion, he said that he knew that he was the only C.P. member amongst the stewards, but that there were 'a few' other members amongst both workers and the management. There was no reference to 'Trots' or any similar group by any person at the factory.

G   Bonus Disputes in the Spare Parts Department

The spare parts department occupied a fairly extensive corner of the main factory building, together with some sheds in the yard outside and a few small sub-stores scattered about the premises. The work in the department could be divided into three roughly defined categories. Firstly, 'indoor' storemen packed away into roof-high racks of bins the many thousands of smaller parts and components which came from suppliers or from other departments. But most of their working time was spent on the selection of items from the bins according to 'order' forms which specified customers' requirements. Then there were packers, who either constructed, or packed parts into, large containers which were sent mostly to the firm's overseas distributors. The packers included several women amongst their number and these workers made parcels of the smaller parts to be sent through the post or for dispatch by air. Thirdly, there were the 'outdoor' storemen who stacked away, or selected and transported between the main stores and the outdoor sheds, the larger components such as axle units, exhaust pipes, silencers, springs, fenders, bonnets, wings etc. There were sixty workers in the department, six junior foremen, a superintendent and his clerk. Working in the stores—but not numbered amongst the department's establishment of sixty—were a fork-lift truck driver, and two paint sprayers who cleaned and re-painted dirty or rusted parts.

A decision to conduct a 'downer'—or small strike—seemed to have its genesis in the discussion of half-a-dozen 'indoor' storemen who were getting ready to go home at the end of the day. A surge of discontent amongst the storemen could be attributed to sharp drops in earnings over three consecutive weeks, and this discontent was transmuted into action by notice of the bonus earnings which could be expected in the pay packets due for distribution on the following day. Details of the bonus calculations had appeared on the departmental notice board late in the afternoon, as was customary, but 'washing up' allowed insufficient time for a plan of action to be defined, and the factory hooter ended discussion. In the morning, this small group informed one of the department's two shop stewards that they required an immediate shop meeting, donned their dustcoats, and as the starting hooter sounded, walked through the stores into the yard, calling on others to join them. If not out of the gates, they were at least out of the workplace and acting collectively to gain something from the management. Technically, they were on strike.

There had been no meeting of the shop to 'authorise' this action: it was itself both a protest and a request for a meeting. Within five minutes, all workers in the department had gathered outside, one steward had gone to find his convener, and the other steward addressed the assembly.

They were told that they had now expressed their protest and should decide to start work and come out again in two hours (when there was an official tea break, although he did not specifically mention this), by which time it was hoped that the convener would be available to come to the meeting. The steward said he had heard that other day-workers were holding similar meetings and that this was why the convener could not come to the meeting immediately. He stressed that his suggestion would be the 'correct' procedure to adopt (though in terms of the engineering disputes procedure this was hardly so). This advice was immediately and vigorously opposed by two of the original small group who had led the way into the yard. They held that unless the workers stayed out to demonstrate that they were acting seriously, they would achieve nothing. No one moved the motion to return to work, and by general assent it was agreed to remain in the yard until the convener could be present.

An hour and a half elapsed before he arrived, and during this time cliques gathered for warmth and shelter in sunny corners about the yard. It was not the weather that was keeping them outside: a few lucky individuals managed to squeeze themselves into an adjacent boiler-house. But it was possible for the researcher to circulate from group to group and absorb information. It was clear that not everybody knew, or was agreed upon, the aims of the strike. Some could express no more than that they were protesting at the drop in the level of the bonus; others assumed that they would be demanding an immediate increase in bonus payments as an interim measure. Perhaps the majority was now acting specifically to force the management to take rapid steps to implement an agreement made fourteen months earlier. This agreement was about the development of a separate bonus scheme for the department, and its negotiation had itself been accompanied by 'downers'. The strike, then, could not be taken in isolation, but was an integral part of a series of downers over issues arising from the bonus payment system.

The day-workers' bonus arrangements have already been described. The spare parts department was especially liable to fluctuations in the level of bonus which bore little relation to variations in the aggregate work load of the department itself. Not only was there no perceptible connection between the output of cars and workloads in these stores, but work stoppages or short-time working elsewhere in the factory, for example, affected weekly output and hence the level of bonus earnings of the storemen. At these times the flow of supplies coming into the factory remained fairly constant and had to be handled. The intake of some supplies into the spares stores thus became greater, and the additional work-load continued while the supplies were transferred into production departments again. However, the storemen emphasised the problems of earnings rather than work-load fluctuations: these constituted a grievance of long standing. The agreement of fourteen months earlier had provided that management undertake work study with the aim of placing each day-work department on what was ambiguously called an 'individual' incentive scheme designed to relate departmental effort more closely with earnings. The operation was to be completed within eighteen months of the agreement. Some other stores had been work-studied, and had been withdrawn from the existing scheme applicable to all day-workers into a bonus scheme of their own. Their earnings had increased: this was common knowledge, and they were envied. In at least one case, the transfer was believed (almost certainly validly) to have been hastened by the use of tactical downers.

Restlessness had increased in the departments which had still to be studied. The stewards in the spares stores, for example, had pressed the superintendent for action on several occasions, but without apparent result. Production holdups, and three consecutive reductions in the level of bonus payments, then coincided with a rumour that two of the firm's three work study engineers who were engaged on the development of the bonus schemes were leaving at the end of that week—'because they were underpaid', it was added. The rumour had some substance: the convener, when he arrived, confirmed that the men were leaving the firm, although their reasons for doing so could not be ascertained.

The convener assumed charge of the meeting, and spoke first of the other meetings he had just been attending. This was an acknowledgment of the real discontents of the day-workers. He was chairman of the J.S.S.C., and said that he had already arranged for a meeting of the Conveners' Committee with the management for that afternoon to discuss the issues which had arisen during the morning. Stoppages on this scale—there had, it seemed, been six other meetings—could scarcely be the concern of one union only, and the issues would be taken up directly with the Personnel Executive. At this, there were mutterings amongst those assembled that the department's particular interests would 'get lost' in a meeting with general terms of reference. Action was wanted at the departmental level, for it was thought that without pressure, the agreement would not be implemented in the few months still available for it to be carried out. The convener then spoke of this agreement of fourteen months before, and said that he would specifically take up with management the matter of delay in its implementation. He followed this with a recommendation that the meeting resolve to return to work—at which discussion became very lively, and different views became more clearly expressed than hitherto.

The first request was for an explanation of the bonus movements. Production figures and the bonus payments for the previous three weeks were read out from the floor: the level of bonus appeared to fall off although production was rising, and the point was made with heavy sarcasm. The effect was due to the time-lag built into bonus calculations, but, in detailed application, these calculations were complicated. When pressed to explain them in detail, the convener said that he was unable to do so. Whether this inability was genuine or merely assumed for the occasion is a moot point: a detailed explanation would have been out of place and unproductive.

Suggestions from the floor that management be asked for an immediate increase in bonus payments were then side-stepped by the convener: they clearly did not have the backing of a majority. The earnings differentials between piece-workers and day workers were then spoken of with some acrimony: the high earnings of piece-workers were envied, and the latter were accused of being uninterested in the problems of day-workers, while piece-workers' actions were often the direct cause of the day-workers' bonus fluctuations. The remarks were aimed at the convener, as he and all members of the Conveners' Committee were held to represent 'piece-workers'.(1) It was clear from the course of the proceedings that neither the departmental stewards nor the convener enjoyed the confidence of the department on this issue or, as it later transpired, more generally.

A pertinent but unhelpful discussion then arose in connection with the agreement of more than a year before. Some workers held that the departmental meeting which had then accepted the agreement had been unrepresentative—even 'rigged' by the stewards to comply with the advice of the convener. It appeared that there had in fact been more than one meeting, involving a reversal of decision—but clarification of this matter could not have been expected at the present stage. Side-issues were being introduced, and the meeting was losing cohesion and becoming mainly a means of relieving pent-up emotions. For example, one of the paint sprayers used the opportunity to raise an individual grievance he had about faulty union communications. He was firmly admonished by the convener for raising an irrelevant matter, and also for having no right to be at the meeting at all as he was not a part of the department's formal establishment. A resolution calling for a return to work was then moved from the floor, was seconded and passed unanimously. The strike had lasted for about two-and-a-half hours, and the return to work was just in time for the tea-break.

On the following day, the departmental stewards 'reported back' the results of the conveners' meeting with management. A meeting of the department was held during the dinner-break, when it was stated that management had at first offered no alleviation of the situation. But negotiations with the management were then still continuing, and it was formally resolved to meet again early in the afternoon, and—if no progress had been made—to go home at 3.00 p.m. as a further protest. The second report-back meeting (at 2.00 p.m. and technically a strike) was

---

(1) The accusation was made by day-workers on other occasions—both publicly and privately. In the context, 'piece-workers' referred to trackmen as well as to workers on individual incentive payment systems. There was no constitutional basis for the accusation, and this was the reply made by the conveners to the charge at one large-scale meeting of day-workers. That all the conveners would be piece-workers was a statistical likelihood: the day-workers were mostly members of the T.G.W.U. There seemed to be several reasons why the T.G.W.U. convener was not a day-worker. Firstly, day-workers elected a minority of the union's departmental stewards. Secondly, the day-workers' stewards seemed generally less active in union affairs than the piece-worker's stewards. Thirdly, within the T.G.W.U. membership at the factory the day-workers were in many departments, and were thus likely to lack cohesion as a group. The paintshops had the largest concentration of T.G.W.U. members: these were 'piece-workers' and, in fact, the T.G.W.U. convener had risen from their number. A number of other factors could influence the election of conveners—not the least of which would, of course, be personal competence.

told that management had offered to recruit four work study engineers as soon as possible. This was held by the workers to be insufficient evidence of progress.

The stewards pointed out that the conveners were themselves recommending a mass meeting of all day-workers in the factory's car park on the following Monday morning (this was a Friday), and that the department stay at work during the afternoon. This recommendation was immediately opposed by one storeman, on the grounds that their problems would 'get lost' at a mass meeting, and that two matters should be pursued by the department independently of any mass action. The two matters which he suggested were, firstly, pressing for the separate bonus scheme, and then also for 'something to make up wages in the meantime'. The departmental stewards were not 'giving a lead', and it had to be reluctantly drawn out of them by close questioning that they themselves favoured acting separately as a department and going home—as had been resolved earlier. In the course of what amounted to an interrogation by one of their members, they both admitted to having no confidence in the Conveners' Committee (in total—as it seemed). A vote was taken on a motion that the department go home at 3.00 p.m., and attend the mass meeting on the Monday as well—all overtime working during the week-end being also explicitly banned. Only a handful of people voted against this motion. (1)

The meeting on the Monday morning was attended by about 600 day-workers. A public address system had been borrowed for the purpose from the T.G.W.U. office. After a general review of the position by the chairman of the Conveners' Committee, (2) and a period of hot and inevitably disjointed discussion (during which two of the 'informal leaders' in the spare parts department—but not the departmental stewards—had spoken), the recommendation of the conveners was for a return to work to allow negotiations to proceed. It was stressed that management would refuse to negotiate until there was a return. The conveners would then press for rapid action by management on the development of departmental bonus schemes, and also take up the possibility of an interim pay increase for day-workers. The recommendation was discussed: on balance, the day-workers seemed to favour a continued 'show of strength' and a demand for higher pay immediately. A motion to stay out on strike but to meet again on the Wednesday morning was carried by a large majority. The matter of a venue was raised as the meeting was breaking up. The conveners suggested the car park again—but that if the firm refused permission, the meeting would be held in the street outside the factory gates. It was noted that this would effectively block the flow of traffic into and out of that part of the factory. It was implied that permission would obviously be forthcoming.

---

(1) When leaving the stores at 3.00 p.m., there was an attempt to 'clock off'—to comply with this management rule for leaving the factory early. But the action was apparently unexpected, as that week's clock cards had already been replaced by those for the following week.

(2) This was before the appointment of the Industrial Relations Officer.

The meeting on the Wednesday seemed less lively. The main point made by the conveners was that management had refused to negotiate. The day-workers eventually accepted their recommendation to return to allow negotiations to proceed—with the rider that there be a further mass meeting in a fortnight to review progress on the main issue i.e. the bonus system. There were no motions at this Wednesday meeting about a straight wage increase or an interim increase in the bonus payments. What was particularly noticeable about these large, open-air strike meetings of day-workers from many departments, was the number of different viewpoints and grievances which were ventilated, and which became embodied in a complicated structure of motions, amendments and rescissions. At one stage in the proceedings, after a vote had been taken, there was confusion about what had in fact been put to the vote: there was no written record of it, nor could the mover be persuaded to repeat it. Particular problems had, of necessity, to become diffused into a lowest common denominator. In practice, this meant that many resolutions were a compromise even before they were taken into negotiation with the management—which may have partially accounted for what seemed to be a persistent residuum of discontent and disillusion with the human and organisational machinery of industrial relations at the factory. This was what the spares storemen meant when they spoke of their problems 'getting lost' at mass meetings.

The mass meeting of day-workers to review progress did not in fact take place. A meeting of the shop stewards representing day-workers had decided—not without opposition from amongst their number—that the resolution had been to hold a mass meeting only 'failing satisfactory progress'. No further downers had taken place in the spares department during the two weeks, and the superintendent had indicated that the work study men were expected to arrive within a matter of days. They moved into the stores on the day before the mass meeting was scheduled —which led some of the storemen to wonder whether it would still take place. The stewards called a meeting of the department during the dinner-break and explained what had been decided at their meeting the day before. They asked that their report be accepted, and that it be agreed that there would be no mass meeting on the following day, for management had said that the number of work study engineers was being doubled again to eight, and that this could be regarded as satisfactory progress. Some of the storemen expressed their indignation at what they regarded as the high-handed alteration of the resolution of a mass meeting. It was suggested that 'present company excepted, the stewards mislead us. They tell us just what they want us to know'. This point having been made, the stewards' report to the meeting was then accepted without opposition. The meeting had extended past the dinner-break by two minutes, and the stewards hastened proceedings, saying that they got into trouble with management when meetings over-ran time.

In their outcome, the downers which had taken place in the spares stores were seen to be effective—in the sense that work study engineers moved into the department within three weeks of the first strike recounted above. Further downers then undoubtedly hastened the appearance of their report. Although the storemen believed the spares department to be a very profitable section of the firm, this was not used explicitly as an argument for applying the pressure of downers. For there was a more general belief in the stores and the factory at large—the evidence cited for it being that of experience—that without pressure in the form of downers or strikes, demands or protests received little attention from management. The obverse belief was expressed by groups of supervisors and individual managers: demands from workers had to be opposed on principle 'or things would soon get out of hand'.

The stoppages of work in the spares department lend themselves to wider generalisation, but some of the more important features may be noted here. Firstly, the issues involved were not frivolous. Nor was the action an outcome of irrationality or hot temper. Although storemen were relatively low-paid in comparison with other workers in the factory, it was less the general level of their earnings than the latters' variability which was leading to active dissatisfaction. Secondly, the unrest was on the shop floor. The stewards attempted to act constitutionally and raise the issue of delay with management. When this failed, and their members took strike action, they attempted to obtain a return to work. They were under pressure from their members, and their leadership appeared reluctant. Thirdly, the stewards and the workers wished to contain or process the issue narrowly within the department. The issue was theirs primarily, and only incidently was it regarded as a general or wage-structural problem of the day-workers in the factory and capable of longer-term solution as such. The 'solidarity' of the department was both of an active kind which would deliberately absorb the personal loss of wages in order to achieve a goal, and of a more passive kind Storemen would not 'black' when others went out on strike, and would even on occasion support trackmen by sympathetic action (although sometimes grudgingly).

The strikes had achieved their immediate objective, and without attempting a typology of strikes, something could be said here about 'downers' generally. They were departmental actions in which both the issues involved and the range of 'solidarity' were narrowly regarded by the workers. They were temporary in a more immediate sense than strikes are usually regarded as being: lines of communication between men and management remained short. The strikers did not 'clock off' or leave the premises (unless there was no convenient meeting place other than the street outside the factory gates). Downers could be called off within a matter of minutes, whereas strikes in which men leave the premises have usually to last for at least the rest of the day or shift. (Downers taking place near the end of the day could, of course, easily be 'go home' strikes.) Downers were 'attention getters' rather than actions to obtain general economic concessions. They seemed to be a form of 'brinkmanship', and conveners gave them priority and moved with speed to achieve a return to work, whereas once men had gone home, discussions and negotiations could be less urgently conducted. Finally, management did not usually 'refuse to negotiate under duress' when there were downers: this seemed to be a tactic for use mainly at the higher levels of procedure for settling disputes, and when issues were already 'clarified' or a firm stand was being taken.

The mass meetings, as they were in fact used, were inappropriate devices for securing a solution to the immediate problems confronting the day-workers. Mass meetings are inevitably clumsy or blunt social instruments: they are useful for general 'reporting back', for issues concerning a whole factory (such as large-scale short-time working), or to raise or demonstrate sympathy. No attempt was made by the conveners at the mass meetings to derive or propagate the generality underlying the cluster of related grievances which had arisen—i.e., the unsuitability of the output-related bonus payments to these day-workers. The mass meetings should not have occurred: the observer gained the impression that they had been forced on the conveners by the sheer pressure of events and the inadequacy of the procedures for handling grievances expeditiously.

H   The 'Breach of Procedure' Strike

This was the largest of the strikes which took place at the factory during the period of the study, in the sense that it accounted for a 'loss' of about 8,500 working days. It is a useful instance of the influence of 'personalities' in some strike situations, of the way in which issues may change from stage to stage in the procedure for settling disputes, of the working of the procedures themselves, and of the occurrence of muddle or misunderstanding. Members of a union of metal workers and mechanics which had only a minority membership in this factory, objected to management's method of investigating the possibility of employing additional metal fitters, and subsequently, the Conveners' Committee demanded the removal of what they regarded as a provocative notice concerning the dispute. Because the dispute occurred during the early part of the observer's period at the factory, the negotiations could not be directly observed. However, lengthy accounts—both written and verbal—were later obtained from conveners and management to supplement the inadequate information available to an 'ordinary' worker during the course of the strike itself. It was, in any case, an involved affair.

The metal fitters operated a 'closed shop' in the main areas in which they were employed, including the brass shop. The firm customarily indented for this type of labour only through the trade union office. The dispute arose initially when management tried to recruit four additional metal fitters for the brass shop. Supervision in that department approached the convener to inform him of the decision to recruit the additional labour—a decision which was immediately opposed. The convener's opposition was based on his desire to protect the earnings of his members in the brass shop which would, in all likelihood, have been affected by reduced overtime working, if not also by the higher number of workers amongst whom bonus earnings would have had to be apportioned. The convener was newly-elected and, to consolidate his position, felt he must maintain or boost the earnings of his members. Manning was subject to negotiation, and he asked that management provide 'facts and figures' about work schedules—i.e. to justify its case for additional labour. There was no formal 'failure to agree', and the matter rested for the time being. But there were already background circumstances which made hostility and misunderstanding likely.

Firstly, it transpired that the Personnel Executive had, about two weeks before, been telephoned by an official of the union. The official was prospecting for jobs for some of his members whom he thought might be made redundant at another firm. The question of additional labour in the brass shop had not yet arisen at the time of the call, and the Personnel Executive was non-committal in his reply. It appears also that the new convener had not, at the time, been informed by his official of this telephone call—an unusual circumstance, due perhaps to the recency of his election. Secondly, the convener had been elected to fill the office just vacated by the new Industrial Relations Officer. There was a heritage of rivalry for the office of convener, and personal animosity, between the Industrial Relations Officer and the new convener. Both of these persons were spoken of by many at the factory as having aggressive, extroverted, and even 'over-bearing' characters. A 'personality clash' was thus one of the popular explanations offered for this strike from its earliest stages. Thirdly, and despite the sanguine attitude of the other conveners to the Industrial Relations Officer's appointment, the metal workers' and mechanics' convener and his members were already prepared to suspect that the Industrial Relations Officer would—as they put it—'try something on'. There was also some degree of indignation on the shop floor generally at the 'defection' of the Industrial Relations Officer, and a strong similar feeling amongst departmental stewards. For example, two thirds of those attending a J.S.S.C. meeting had voted against any expression of appreciation to this ex-chairman of their committee for his past services.

The issue then became one of a 'breach of procedure'. When informed of the convener's opposition to the recruitment of extra metal fitters, the Industrial Relations Officer telephoned the union official 'for a friendly chat in an informal capacity' (as he put it). As a result of this call, the official arrived at the factory to discuss the matter with his convener. From the latter's point of view, the visit was unexpected. The official had in fact been asked for labour by the Industrial Relations Officer. This approach to the union official on a matter which had not yet passed beyond shop-floor levels was to the convener a clear 'breach of procedure'—i.e. of informal or customary procedure—as the firm could be held to have the right to employ the men under the 'managerial functions' provisions of formal 'Procedure'.(1)

About two days had elapsed since the issue of extra labour had first been raised with the convener, and he decided to call a meeting of his committee. The committee decided that he should ask for a formal meeting with the Industrial Relations Officer—the terms of reference being the latter's 'breach of procedure'—and that two committeemen should accompany the convener. The committeemen worked in the brass shop and, when asked to convene the meeting, the Industrial Relations Officer assumed that the matter was still specifically a brass shop issue and arranged that the meeting be held in the brass shop superintendent's office. When advised of the arrangement, the convener would not accept the presence of any of the brass shop supervision at this meeting. To him, the matter was no longer a brass shop concern, and the presence of two committeemen was a matter of trade union protection. The convener did not yet feel secure enough to meet the Industrial Relations Officer on his own, but the Industrial Relations Officer would not accept a situation where he

_____

(1) At later discussions during the dispute it was argued that the Industrial Relations Officer had acted unusually, also, by arranging an employment matter—an 'interference' with the functions of the Employment Officer which the latter resented and resisted.

was to be outnumbered by three to one. A number of alternative possibilities were rejected by one party or the other, because—as it seemed—they either required the presence of brass shop supervision or the absence of the metal fitters' committeemen. Misunderstanding about exactly what alternatives had been suggested or rejected arose later as an important factor in the continuance of the dispute. The main issue was now the constitution of a joint meeting, and it was at this stage that work stoppages began to occur.

On the next morning—the third day of the dispute—the metal fitters' committee decided to call a meeting of all their members in the factory during the dinner-break, both to inform them of the situation and to arrange for some form of pressure to be put upon the management. This meeting was held on the factory premises, overran starting time by fifteen minutes, and became, technically a strike. The workers endorsed their convener's insistence on the presence of his committeemen at a meeting with the Industrial Relations Officer, but at the same time, decided that a meeting which would include the brass shop superintendent was in order as far as they were concerned. However, a ban on overtime working was called for the following day (Saturday) in reprisal for the Industrial Relations Officer's refusal to meet the convener and committeemen on the previous day. Thus, men on the shop floor supported some action by their representatives, but altered its direction.

Work at the factory continued normally throughout the following Monday, but a new twist was given to the wrangling over an acceptable constitution for the requested meeting. After obtaining the assurance of the union official that there was no standing ban on overtime by the metal fitters, and knowing that a meeting which would include both brass shop supervision and the Union's committeemen would now be acceptable to the metal fitters, management duly arranged a meeting to be held early in the afternoon.

However, because the Personnel Executive had been a party to telephone conversations with the union official about the dispute, management decided that he should now also attend the meeting. The convener did not yet know of this.

On arrival at the venue, the convener and his committeemen objected to the attendance of the Personnel Executive. His presence at the meeting was held to be yet a further 'breach of procedure', because a meeting with the Personnel Executive formed the last stage in domestic procedure. Management explained the informal capacity of the Personnel Executive—as a relevant party to a number of telephone conversations with the union official. The objection stood: the presence of the Personnel Executive at this meeting could be held to bias him if the matter had to be taken to his stage of procedure. Neither side would bend, so the meeting did not take place. According to the Industrial Relations Officer, Management 'consistently argued the right to have in attendance at the meeting members of their own choice, and accepted that the union had the same right'.

The convener asked for—and was refused—permission to hold a meeting of his members at starting-time in the morning. The meeting was held outside the factory gates. The union's factory committee met beforehand, accepted the convener's suggestion to conduct a 'sit-down' action, the meeting was addressed to this effect and the metal fitters went to their workplaces and stood about for the rest of the morning. The convener later explained the tactics of a 'sit-down' strike: his members were available for work 'at one minute's notice'. The union's committee was clearly hoping that this pressure would be effective, and that the strikers would be back at work during the afternoon. The metal fitters had decided to meet again to review the position during the dinner-break.

By mid-morning, metal fitters at the firm's main engine factory had joined in the strike, management had laid-off about 1, 400 workers for the rest of the day, and the Conveners' Committees of both factories had been given permission to hold meetings of all shop stewards. The Conveners' Committee at the assembly factory had—of course—kept in constant touch with events, and now formally entered the situation, as their members were being directly affected by the dispute. Hourly-paid workers in the factory could be laid off work at one hour's notice; and if the lay-off was in consequence of a strike at the establishment, there was no obligation on the part of the firm to give such notice or to operate the 'guaranteed week' agreement.(1) The men laid off on this occasion in fact waited about the factory for a further hour after the notice had become effective, in the hope that a solution to the dispute might be found, and to await the report back of their stewards. The J.S.S.C. meeting could do little but exchange and clarify information. By about noon it was clear that no progress would be made that day: the men waiting about were leaving the factory, and, at their 'review' meeting, the metal fitters decided to continue their strike at home. Management had refused to consider arranging an acceptable joint meeting while there was a 'sit-down'.

By this time, repercussions of the strike had spread beyond even those departments which had been laid off for the rest of the day—quite apart from the inevitable effect on the bonus earnings of both management and men. For example, two unauthorised shop floor meetings had been hurriedly called in the spare parts department during the morning, the first of these by the informal leaders who 'guided' the bonus dispute meetings already recounted. At this first meeting, the departmental stewards were censured for not having 'reported back' to the department after the J.S.S.C. meeting that morning, and further, for not recommending a sympathetic strike by the storemen if the trackmen were, in fact, to go home. 'Sympathy' was only a secondary consideration: it was made quite explicit that the action would be a protest at the drop in bonus earnings which would result from the reduced output of cars. The second meeting followed on within an hour of the first—and after most of the trackmen had left the factory. The deputy convener of the T.G.W.U. arrived in the department, called the meeting, and said that the metal fitters did not in fact want support at that stage. He had clearly been told of the earlier

---

(1) The 'guaranteed week' agreement was automatically suspended, but management usually gave the one hour's notice. Managers and stewards said that the one hour's notice could be used as a 'duress' measure i.e. the management's equivalent of a 'downer'.

meeting, and advised the storemen to remain at work to allow the work study engineers (then in the department) to continue their observations. This advice was accepted without the need for a vote. These two meetings demonstrated a point that stewards and conveners often made privately: that their main efforts were directed towards keeping men at work, not taking them out on strike.

On the Wednesday morning, the metal fitters continued their 'sit-down' on the premises. Their convener and a committeeman were formally reporting the situation to the Conveners' Committee when a warning was received from the Industrial Relations Officer that unless normal working was resumed by the metal fitters, trackmen would be sent home within an hour. To attempt to resolve the situation, the full Conveners' Committee then met the Industrial Relations Officer, the progress of the dispute was reviewed, and it appeared that there had been misunderstanding (1) about the proffered forms of meeting at an earlier stage. However, there was now no objection by the metal fitters' convener or the Industrial Relations Officer to the holding of a meeting on the issue of 'breach of procedure by the Industrial Relations Officer' at the last stage of domestic procedure, i.e. at the Personnel Executive's level. With this agreed, the convener immediately telephoned through to the relevant departments for his members to resume work, a J.S.S.C. meeting (authorised by management and standing by) was informed of the situation, and the management arranged for the 'breach of procedure' meeting to be held at 4.15 that afternoon—at which officials of the metal fitters' union were to be present at the request of their convener. The immediate crisis appeared to be over.

However, the Personnel Executive and Industrial Relations Officer now felt that they had been out-manoeuvred by the stewards. In a later letter to the employers' association, they wrote of having been informed that morning of considerable confusion in the minds of employees at both factories affected as to the truth of the affair, and that the confusion was made worse by a rapidly growing rumour that management had been made to 'climb down' because of the strike. Accordingly, and in close consultation with the Group Director, an official notice (over the signature of the Industrial Relations Officer) was prepared and posted on all factory notice boards during the early part of the afternoon. The notice read:

> Once again there has been a futile unofficial stoppage of work, and the only winners from the outcome are our competitors. To avoid

---

(1) The 'misunderstanding' deserves a further word. Such matters are difficult to clarify: each side impugned the honour of the other. Misunderstanding was—under the circumstances—not improbable. The Industrial Relations Officer's actual role in procedure was not at this stage clear to the conveners. Also the dialogue dealing with the various alternative meetings seemed to have been brief, heated and unbending. Two of the conveners said later that they felt that the offer of the disputed alternative (i.e. a meeting at the last stage of domestic procedure) may have been made by the Industrial Relations Officer to the union's official during a telephone conversation that day—and not to the union's convener.

any misunderstandings which may exist regarding the circumstances the Company wish to make clear the following points. 1. The Company at no time refused to convene a meeting. The Company only refused to call a meeting in conditions where the eligibility of management personnel to attend the meeting was to be decided solely by the union concerned. The management maintain an equal right with the union to select their own representatives in accordance with established procedure, custom and practice. 2. Following upon a resumption of normal working this morning the union concerned intimated willingness to accept the constitution of a meeting in a form offered by the Company last Thursday [six days before]. Accordingly this meeting will take place today constituted exactly in a form which was refused by the union concerned last Thursday.

The notice was clearly important for the status of the new Industrial Relations Officer. Its effects on the shop stewards were almost immediate—and could have been predicted. The Combine Committee was already in session, being consulted by the metal fitters' conveners in preparation for the coming meeting, when it was informed by two departmental stewards that a notice had been put up. There was an adjournment to read it. The metal fitters' convener called his union committee together: a decision was taken to call the metal fitters out on strike, but that they should be at their workplaces again in the morning. These workers left the factory within a short while of the posting of the notice. The Combine Committee meanwhile reconvened to decide the next step. At 4.00 p.m. the chairman and secretary asked the Industrial Relations Officer to have the notice withdrawn immediately as being 'provocative and ill-timed'. There could be no agreement: the stewards formally registered 'failure to agree' and asked for a meeting with the Personnel Executive. This took place within a few minutes: discussion was brief, heated and unproductive, and was closed by the Personnel Executive.

The meeting planned for 4.15 p.m. did not take place: neither conveners nor union officials put in an appearance. At 4.30 p.m. the Combine Committee requested a meeting of the whole committee with the Personnel Executive—a move interpreted by the management as being one to gain the tactical advantage of numbers. The management team—consisting of the Personnel Executive and the Industrial Relations Officer—was thus increased to include the Personnel Officer of the engine factory. The meeting lasted over two hours, and ended without substantive result. But it was agreed to reconvene in the morning to continue discussion on removal or retention of the notice. It was agreed also to follow on in the morning with another meeting to discuss both the contents of the notice and the original 'breach of procedure' issue. The metal fitters' conveners, mindful of union autonomy and strength of numbers, now asked to have the Combine Committee 'sitting in' on discussions at the follow-on meetings. This was agreed by management and the Combine Committee.

At starting time on the Thursday morning—as the adjourned meeting was about to recommence—one of the union's officials obtained permission for a private word with the Combine Committee. There is some doubt about whether permission was then requested for a meeting of the metal fitters, and if so, whether this was refused by the management. In any event, the convener called his members outside the gates to be addressed by their official, while the Combine Committee was to continue the meeting with management. However, management felt that this latest adjournment had been used to stage a strike, and refused to meet until the men had resumed work. The official was informed, and replied by saying that his members would not resume work unless the notice was withdrawn. This pressure was withstood, and the official then persuaded his members to return to work. The factory worked normally for the rest of that day. It was clear that management's determination to withstand strike action had been tested.

The adjourned meeting thus began in mid-morning and lasted, off and on, until about 7.00 p.m. From the beginning, the stewards remained firm on the terms of reference: that the immediate source of irritation was the 'provocativeness and ill-timing' of the notice. The content was not now at issue: this was a metal fitters' matter and only the removal of the notice would allow discussion on the validity of its contents to be held. The situation was fraught with frustrations. Management explained that they had not wished to give the impression of being provocative, and that, provided the stewards would agree that the validity of the notice was unchallenged, it could be removed and some other notice could be substituted. The stewards, on their part, were pressing for removal of the notice in a way which would not prejudice subsequent discussion about its validity.

Draft notices flowed into wastepaper baskets in the conference room: two of these are sufficient to illustrate the form the arguments were taking. Management proposed a notice which read:

> The Company was requested to withdraw the notice posted yesterday (stating the facts in connection with the recent dispute) on the grounds that it is provocative and ill-timed. The Company does not wish to appear provocative and on the clear understanding that the accuracy of the notice is unchallenged the Company agree to its withdrawal. The Company wishes to make it clear that the sole intention of the previous notice was to ensure that the true facts were known to all employees.

This draft was rejected by the Combine Committee on the grounds that it left little for discussion at the subsequent meeting. They rejected, also, a management suggestion that a stewards' notice be placed alongside the offending one provided it was 'factual' on the grounds that, until the next meeting had been held, they did not have the facts. The stewards proposed a notice reading:

> Whilst the validity of this statement has not been challenged at this stage it has been withdrawn whilst negotiations take place.

Management felt that this draft would not cover the situation because the words 'at this stage' could be construed to mean that the contents of the notice were not valid. Stewards replied by accusing the management of 'playing with words'.

At the end of the day's discussion it was agreed to meet again in the morning, but the Combine Committee decided to break what appeared as a deadlock. The chairman and secretary returned after a few minutes to the conference room, and asked for an immediate answer as to whether the notice was to be withdrawn or not. From the stewards' point of view, the issue was perishable. If the notice was not to be removed soon, there was little point in removing it at all. Management withstood this pressure, holding that it was necessary to reach mutual agreement on a revised notice. The matter would be considered closed unless the stewards agreed to resume discussions on these terms in the morning. This reply ended the day's deliberations.

Strike action began again on the Friday morning. Metal fitters met outside the gates of both main factories, and decided to withdraw their labour. They went home, having arranged to meet again on the following Monday morning at a public park in the city. Fifteen hundred workers at the factory were laid-off for the rest of the day. The Conveners' Committee at the assembly factory held a meeting of the J.S.S.C., at which it was decided to ask union officials for immediate assistance. The Group Director wished to address the assembled shop stewards later in the morning: it was put to the stewards, and was refused on the grounds that 'it would serve no useful purpose as enough damage had been done by the notice'. The notice was of concern to the stewards because, apart from its tone and timing, it was a statement to their members on an issue still under discussion.

Union officials arrived in mid-morning. After meeting the conveners in the conference room, one official—in his capacity as chairman of the District Committee of the C.S.E.U.—called the Group Director on the telephone, asking him to meet the officials then at the factory. The request was refused: it was explained that no negotiation could take place until there was a resumption of work. The official then requested that the notice—the immediate cause of the day's stoppage—should be removed, not as a challenge to its accuracy but to obtain progress. The reply was forthright: unless the validity of the notice could be disproved, it would not under any circumstances be removed, however long the strike might last. The official asked, finally, whether a union notice could be posted alongside the firm's notice. The Group Director pointed out that this facility had been offered to the stewards on the previous day, and had been refused. A union notice would be in order—provided it was accompanied by a statement making it clear that it was being posted in acceptance of an offer by the firm made on the previous day and before the current strike. This proviso could not be acceded to by the officials: negotiation—formal or informal—ended for the day.

Further lay-offs took place, and these workers were advised that, because of the uncertainty of the position, they were to await public announcements about the resumption of working. The trade union officials left the factory after having decided to apply through the employers' association for a meeting with the management. The officials and conveners of the metal fitters' union agreed to call a meeting of the union leadership for the following morning to decide whether or not the strike should be made official. The Conveners' Committee arranged for a meeting of the J.S.S.C. to be held at a working men's club near the public park—before the meeting of strikers and with union officials present.

Later, in the afternoon, management was said to have convened a meeting of all staff members—held in a canteen—to inform them of the position.

The meeting of the union on the Saturday morning was reported to have been lengthy and lively. Eventually, while endorsing the actions of its conveners, the union leadership felt that the issues in dispute—whether of the notice, its contents, or the previous 'breach of procedure'—would not warrant an official strike. The strikers were to be recommended to return to work, and the union was to take the issues directly to the employers' association. The rest of the tale can be briefly told. On the Monday, the J.S.S.C. was vigorously discontented with the turn events had taken: the Conveners' Committee could now scarcely justify any strike action over the notice, and were put in the position of appearing to be ineffective. The J.S.S.C. had had little chance of influencing the conduct of the dispute, many workers had been laid-off, and the stewards would now have to report back to their members that the issue of the notice had been lost.

Stewards and their members spoke of the strike as a defeat: men returned to work on precisely the same terms as they had left it, and the offending notice remained in place on at least some notice boards for several months. The metal fitters duly accepted the recommendation to return to work; and the C.S.E.U. officials no longer felt it necessary to contact the employers' association, as the matter was now being pursued directly by the metal fitters' union. For all practical purposes, the 'breach of procedure' strike was over. There were, it seems, two subsequent meetings—held at the offices of the employers' association—between officials of the union and senior managers of the firm which discussed this dispute. Little information is available about these meetings, and whatever value they might have had as postmortems was not of the kind that was perceptible at shop floor level. The original issue of additional workers in the brass shop never arose again. The employment position had changed, and many workers at the factory were being put onto short-time working.

To attempt to draw up a balance sheet of rights and wrongs in an affair of this kind would be both tedious and unproductive. There are points to be made for and against both sides, and some matters must inevitably remain obscure. In some respects the dispute was atypical: it involved the biggest strike of the period, to start with. But it may be worth recording the prevailing opinion of the conveners in discussing the dispute several months after it had occurred. It was held that, whilst management had been at fault in making a direct approach to the trade union to obtain labour, the issue was scarcely substantial enough to have been allowed to develop into a large-scale stoppage. 'Personalities' explained the escalation: those of the metal fitters' convener and the Industrial Relations Officer in the early stages of the dispute, and that of the Group Director over the matter of works' notices. (1)

─────────────

(1) This view was not accepted by the Industrial Relations Officer when reading an earlier draft of this account of the strike. However, inarticulate premises of the 'personality' explanation were the conjunction of the particular situations in which the leading personalities found themselves, and the vagueness of the disputes procedure.

The conveners felt that they—collectively—bore much of the onus of the defeat in the eyes of their members, and held that the dispute had contributed substantially to the general weakening of their control over departmental stewards and their members during the period of the study. The metal fitters' convener, for his part, was still a little 'touchy' or defensive about his role in the affair: he held that the strike had at least demonstrated that his members were still strongly organised despite the 'defection' of their previous convener. He reported a subsequent spirit of 'full cooperation' on the part of the supervisors with whom he dealt.

Perhaps the most important point which was demonstrated by the affair was the uncertainty of the conveners' powers of intervention in 'single-union' issues, and the difficulty they had in deciding at just what stage such issues justified action by the Conveners' Committee. The problem was not a new one to the conveners: they had spoken to the researcher of earlier occasions when consideration for individual union autonomy had led them to stand back at times when they considered that they could otherwise have intervened to the general advantage. The problem had its genesis in the presence of several unions at the factory, but it can be suggested that a solution does not necessarily depend on the adoption of industrial or plant unionism. A more practical possibility could be the formulation of a domestic procedure specifying participation by the conveners jointly, and involving the individual unions' officials only at the 'official' stages.

I   The Solidarity or Reprisal Strike

This strike was the largest but one of all the strikes which occurred
during the course of the study: although short and sharp, it was large in
terms both of numbers of workers involved and the total of striker-days.
The factory was in effect shut down for two days. As in the case of the
'breach of procedure' affair, this dispute took place while the observer
was working on the shop floor, and originated in a department not at that
time open to a 'participant' enquirer. Direct observation of negotiations
and the early stages was thus again rather limited. Reliance has had to
some extent to be placed on partial accounts of the affair gathered at
later periods during the field-work. However, the main purpose of the
account which follows is to demonstrate not so much the substantive issue
over which the strike originated, or even the detailed course of the events
themselves, as the matrix of insecurity of employment and earnings in
which it was shaped and a weakening of the shop steward organisation.
In a context of increasing shop-floor discontent, the conveners found
themselves unable to control a movement for militant action initiated by
some departments and their stewards.

'Waiting-time', short-time working, and an accumulation of unfinished
cars about the factory premises, were the most salient background factors in the genesis of the strike. Two months prior to the main events,
and shortly after the Group Director's return from a visit to the firm's
main overseas markets, an official notice had been posted about the factory. The notice drew attention to the fact that many complaints about
the quality of the firm's products had been made to the Group Director
while he had been overseas, and that the standards of inspection had had
to be raised. The notice acknowledged that the effects of the campaign
for higher quality had led to a fall in the level of production, and it was
regretted that earnings had also consequently fallen. It was from about
the time of the posting of this notice, also, that rumours began circulating
about the factory—carrying the 'authority' of clerical employees in the
Sales Department—that export orders had dropped away markedly.

The rumours gained credence not only because of an increasing frequency with which assembly workers were held up by shortages of bodies, but
also because of the visible accumulation of cars about the factory. The
cars were not meeting inspection standards at points between the end of
the basic assembly processes and the 'final line', i.e. the department
where the vehicles were cleaned, polished, decked with finery, and adjust-
ed after a roller or road test and before passing to the Dispatch Department for collection by distributors. Faulty paintwork was said to be the
main problem, and the difficulties seemed initially to be concentrated in
a new paint section where cars, already largely assembled, could be re-
painted under low temperature conditions. This 'rectification' took

account both of minor blemishes passed over at earlier stages of the manufacturing process, and of damage incurred during the assembly process itself. These 'paint problems', and the reactions of trade union officials and conveners to them, are mentioned in more detail in the following section of this paper. Here it need only be noted that, by the time of the strike, the number of assembled cars awaiting rectification or minor attention was of the order of two weeks' 'normal' or expected output for the factory. The cars filled an adjacent sportsfield—which came to be called the 'graveyard'—and other spaces about the factory. There were rumours that yet others were accumulating on storage sites away from the factory. They were 'a millstone around the company's neck'—as the Production Manager said to the conveners on one occasion.

The immediate issue at the beginning of the dispute was one of consultation between shop stewards and supervisors in the bodyshop over an alteration which had been made to the amount of waiting-time payment(1) claimed by a gang of eighteen men. The gang stopped work when paysheets for the previous week's work were distributed and it was noticed that an adjustment had been made to the hours of waiting-time which had been booked. The earnings were less than had been expected. The gang contained members of two unions (the N.U.V.B. and the S.M.W.U.) but this strike action took place against the advice of the conveners—who had recommended that a 'failure to agree' be registered with the shop superintendent and thus formally bringing conveners into procedure. It later became apparent that, at this early stage, there was confusion about the exact nature of the men's grievance.

The conveners were at first under the impression that the men had not been consulted about the alteration in the amount of waiting-time payment claimed, and they informed the Industrial Relations Officer about this. The reply received was that—if the men had in fact not been consulted—

---

(1) Workers on assembly tracks could claim a waiting-time payment when they were not able to achieve their 'target' output (and hence 'normal' earnings) due to causes such as mechanical breakdowns, shortage of supplies, or untenable working conditions. There was no timing of periods during which men might be kept involuntarily waiting about for work, but the payment was calculated according to a formula. The number of workers in the department or gang was multiplied by the number of working hours in a 'normal' week, and the resulting figure was divided by the number of cars scheduled to be produced during that week. This calculation produced a figure of 'hours per car' which could be claimed by the department or gang for each car by which the actual production fell short of scheduled production (or pro rata for the period spent at work during the week). However, the rate of pay for these hours was less than half of the average hourly earnings of the men at the time. A claim for an increased rate of waiting-time payment had been formulated and was being put into procedure at the time of the study. It was the belief of some of the conveners and their officials that a higher waiting-time payment would force the firm to improve efficiency, reduce the waiting-time periods, and hence make earnings more stable.

74

the company was in the wrong and that the matter would be put to rights as soon as the men resumed work. Confusion over the exact nature of the grievance could be attributed to the fact that the N.U.V.B. Steward in the bodyshop had been absent on the day before the dispute, that another member of the gang had been informed by supervision of the alteration to the claim, that there was dispute over whether the supervisor had told this member of the gang that the absent steward had previously agreed to the alteration, and that the amount of waiting-time payment which had been claimed was wrong.(1) This latter error was later admitted by the gang and their steward, and the protest of the gang then crystallised around the adequacy of consultation and the statements which had been made by the supervisor. Clarification of these matters took time and remained incomplete. Events were in the meantime being affected by pressure from the side of management.

Within fifteen minutes of the 'downer', most assembly departments (but not the final line or paintshop) had been given an hour's notice of lay-off by the Tracks Executive. There had been one-day lay-offs of individual supply departments during the previous fortnight, as well as frequent periods of waiting-time on the assembly tracks themselves. For example, on the day before the downer by the bodyshop gang, the pre-mount tracks had found themselves waiting for bodies on four separate occasions during the morning,(2) supplemented by a protest stoppage of fifteen minutes during the afternoon—organised by the departmental stewards— over a quite separate issue which had as its basis the facilities granted to shop stewards. Also, both management and stewards had to confront problems created by a downer in the spare parts department (another in the series over the bonus issue) which overlapped with that of the body shop gang.

In response to the downer by the bodyshop gang, the secretary of the J.S.S.C. obtained permission from management to hold a stewards' meet- ing, and asked for suspension of the notice of lay-off while he attempted to get the men (most of whom were members of his union) to return to work. The notice was extended for an hour, and the Industrial Relations Officer stressed that no negotiations on the issue in dispute would be

---

(1) The error in the claim arose out of a perhaps excusable failure to distinguish between the method for calculating bonus payments and that for waiting-time. Under the bonus system, the work of an absentee could be borne by others in the gang and the bonus which he would have earned could be shared between them. The bodyshop gang had a normal complement of nineteen, of whom one had been absent during the week concerned. Waiting-time had been claimed on his behalf—and it was the alteration of this error by supervision that gave rise to dispute about the adequacy of consultation.

(2) On this occasion, one of the pre-mount workers voiced an opinion which was later expressed by some conveners and full-time offi- cials: the management was believed to prefer this waiting-time to an admission of short-time working, because of the presumed ill-effects of this latter on the public—and financial—standing of the firm.

permitted until the men were working again. Attempts to persuade the strikers to return to work failed, and by midday they had gone home. The J.S.S.C. then convened, although in depleted numbers: the pressure of events had left insufficient time for all departmental stewards—particularly those representing dayworkers—to be informed that there was to be a meeting.

It was at this gathering that several track stewards—hard pressed by their members to protest at what they regarded as excessive waiting-time and the unnecessary speed with which lay-offs were taking place—staged a reprisal against the management. A 'one out, all out' motion was put to the meeting, and passed. Although the notice of lay-off had already expired, it was known that the men were waiting at their work-places for their stewards to report back to them. They were to be advised to consider themselves on strike in support of the body-shop strikers, to go home for the rest of the day, but to clock-on for work at the factory on the following morning. The resolution was to apply to other departments which had not been laid-off (and these included the paint shop and final line), but not to departments whose stewards had not been present at the meeting. In fact, no day-workers were directly involved in the strike at this stage. After report-back meetings, the laid-off track workers and others duly went home on strike.

The reprisal policy had not been adopted unanimously at the stewards' meeting: it had been argued that the proposed action would be 'just playing into management's hands'. What seemed to be a growing suspicion on the shop floor—and amongst the stewards—that the cars made at the factory were not then in sufficient demand to warrant the rate of production which had been planned, was used to justify this line of argument. Management was held to be looking for excuses to lay men off work. The conveners, for their part, took the view (which they subsequently stated quite explicitly) that there was nothing which they or the shopfloor could do to induce the continued production of cars which management did not want to produce, and that their efforts in the situation in which they then found themselves were best expended in attempting to keep as many men at work for as long as was possible. This was not an attractive argument to use against those who resented being treated as 'casual labour' (as they saw it). A policy to stop all work in the factory, and not just that which it suited management to halt, had appealed to a majority of the stewards at the meeting. The motion had the appeal of both solidarity and reprisal or counter-attack.

On the following morning—a Friday—whilst all shop stewards were gathering for a full J.S.S.C. meeting, the Conveners' Committee was warned by the Industrial Relations Officer that a general laying-off of trackmen was again imminent. The conveners postponed the J.S.S.C. meeting, and spoke with the bodyshop gang in an attempt to get them to resume work. They failed in this attempt, the body shop gang left the factory an hour or so after the starting hooter had sounded, and the notice of lay-off given to trackmen expired shortly thereafter. The conveners had requested that the lay-off of trackmen be postponed while full-time officials were brought in, but management felt this course to be impractical in the time available. A day had elapsed since the body shop gang had first stopped work. The gang held that adjustments to claims for waiting-time payment should not be made without mutual agreement, that the amount in this instance had been altered without adequate consultation, and (as it was reported later) that supervision had made statements which were untrue. In any event, the men could not be persuaded to return to work.

The 'one out, all out' policy was extended at the J.S.S.C. meeting which then took place. After a brief report by the chairman on the failure of the Conveners' Committee both to obtain a return to work by the body-shop gang and to prevent the immediate laying-off of assembly workers, a motion was moved from the floor (by an N.U.V.B. steward) that the policy of the previous day be put into full effect: that all stewards whose members were still working call meetings and recommend an immediate strike in sympathy with the body-shop gang. The motion was explicit and was unanimously carried: the workers who went on strike were 'giving up as a protest any payment under the guaranteed week agreement, and also the right to unemployment benefit'.(1) The reprisal element still seemed predominant, as the bodyshop gang's grievance was scarcely discussed. The meeting broke up rapidly, and shortly after 9.00 a.m.—by the time the departmental stewards had reported back to their members—the factory was all but deserted.

During the afternoon, full-time officials of the two unions with members in the body shop contacted the director of the employers' association for his assistance in reaching a formula whereby negotiations could take place. These mediatory overtures were unsuccessful: the Works Manager—when approached—informed the director of the association that no negotiations with the unions or the stewards could take place whilst there was an unconstitutional stoppage of work. The conveners had in any case been in a difficult position since the original 'one out, all out' policy had arisen. With the possible exception of the N.U.V.B. convener (who seemed to have been under pressure to demonstrate militancy on account of strong competition for his office from the steward who moved the 'one out, all out' motion), they had neither suggested nor resisted the policy. They had become cautious in opposing strong shop-floor feeling because of criticism of their leadership—which had been voiced on a number of occasions since the 'breach of procedure' affair. This caution had been apparent at the meeting when the policy was extended: they had merely reported on their failure to get a return to work, and made no attempt to offer an alternative to the militants.

The waiting-time issue was settled quite suddenly. Management produced the records of a conference which had been held three years earlier, and in which it had been agreed—inter alia—that in the event of disputes

---

(1) This part of the motion was, of course, rather pious: the guaranteed week agreement is automatically suspended at any establishment where there is a strike, and it is very doubtful whether, in view of the circumstances, those who might have been laid-off by management would have been entitled to claim unemployment benefit under the National Insurance Act.

over waiting-time payment, the lower figure was to be paid pending investigation.(1) The body shop gang had been basing their claim for 'mutual agreement' on a Works Conference decision of over ten years standing which was said to have established that there was to be agreement on waiting-time claims before they were sent to the wages office. When the later agreement was produced at a meeting of the gang early on the following Monday morning, they agreed to resume work—not without criticism of the guidance on this point which they had received from one of the conveners. Within an hour of normal starting time, the gang were back at work, and the assembly tracks had started moving again.

The J.S.S.C. meeting which was convened at noon on the day of the return to work, for the purpose of reviewing the situation, itself illuminated several aspects of industrial relations at the factory. Firstly, this had been the second occasion within two months on which the factory's labour organisation had made a large-scale stand, and been forced to retract (the other being over the 'provocative and ill-timed' notice). The conveners' leadership, or control, had been greatly weakened, and it was not surprising that the conduct of the meeting was boisterous and untidy. The chairman's opening report began with an item which could only have contributed to the emotional tenor of the proceedings. The Group Director had, that morning, and without referring to either supervision or shop stewards, approached and addressed a meeting of inspectors. The inspectors had stopped work in protest against the slow progress being made in regard to changes in their bonus scheme. According to reports, the Group Director had spoken to them with some asperity, had said that he would 'shut the plant down for months' if they did not return to work immediately, and had described the conveners as 'trouble-makers'. He had, it seems, called the conveners together earlier in the day and made much the same points to them more directly. The conveners had decided to refer these charges to their officials.(2)

The next point which the chairman made was that management had told the Conveners' Committee during the morning that workers could expect further short-time working during the week—the reason given by the

---

(1) This works agreement may very well have been in conflict with Section II (1) (a) of the Engineering Procedure Agreement. See A. Marsh, op. cit., pp. 92-94.

(2) The charges were taken sufficiently seriously by full-time officials to raise them formally at a meeting with senior management at the offices of the employers' association. The meeting was said to have achieved no satisfactory result from the unions' point of view in this regard. Thereafter, the conveners decided to attend no meetings at which the Group Director was to be present until an apology had been received from him. However, this policy was not put to the test during the period of study, it was doubtful whether the decision was even communicated to management, and it was not referred to again.

management being a shortage of bodies arising out of the strike. (1) Stewards immediately berated the conveners for their acceptance of this notice of further lay-offs, and there was talk on the floor of the meeting about the possibility of continuing the 'one out, all out' policy. Another steward proposed an 'official enquiry into the mismanagement' of the firm. The conveners replied to the talk about continuation of a 'one out, all out' policy by saying that it would be stupid under the circumstances, that they could not support such a policy, and that there did not seem to be an answer to the prospective laying-off of the tracks. They treated the suggestion of an official enquiry by ignoring it (even though it had been seconded). (2)

The strike and the subsequent return to work were then discussed, the conveners being attacked for inefficient record-keeping. They had had no copy of the agreement which the management had produced as an effective answer to what now appeared to have been the main grievance of the body shop gang. The secretary of the J.S.S.C. replied to this charge by saying that the agreement was only a part of the findings of a Works Conference which had been held on other issues, and that the Industrial Relations Officer had known about it only because he had been the only one of the conveners involved in the issue at the time.(3) The meeting broke up in an atmosphere of general disillusion: the final item was a suggestion from the floor that there was little confidence in the Conveners' Committee amongst the general membership, and that the unwillingness of workers to raise their voluntary contributions to the Shop Stewards' Fund was evidence of this attitude. The suggestion was not taken up by anybody—either in support or in refutation. Over a thousand trackmen were in fact sent home by the management for the afternoon and over fifteen hundred for the following day.

Conveners later spoke individually to the observer of the effects of the increasing shop-floor discontent on their control over the factory's labour organisation. They were not succeeding in their stated policy of keeping as many men at work for as long as possible. The 'one out, all out' resolution was known to have been foolish at the time it was raised.

---

(1) The reason was not questioned at the J.S.S.C. meeting. Although the technicalities were not discussed, the fact that trackmen had remained at work for up to two hours immediately following the initial stoppage, and that there had been technical problems in the paint shop in the days preceding the stoppage, probably made discussion unnecessary.

(2) On other occasions, the conveners spoke of the difficulties of making out a convincing charge of 'mismanagement'.

(3) In later accounts to the observer, management said that the secretary of the J.S.S.C. had been reminded of the agreement when the bodyshop gang first stopped work—i.e. on the Thursday morning. The conveners said that it had not been mentioned until the Friday afternoon, and that, on the Monday morning, they had still not seen a copy of it.

Except for one convener, it seemed that they would have spoken out against the resolution only had they felt that they had the authority to do so effectively. There was evidence to support the conveners' contention that the confidence of workers in their leadership was not readily apparent and was probably declining. Individual criticism, and motions of 'no confidence', made at departmental and J.S.S.C. meetings, have already been referred to. While leaders are always open to such attacks, the impression was that they were occurring more frequently. There was also a noticeable decline over the period of the study in the control of shop stewards' meetings by the conveners (which could not be related merely to the change of chairman). For example, some meetings were poorly attended, and stewards started leaving the meetings early without reference to the platform.

A decline in the administrative efficiency of the factory's labour organisation was both cause and effect of some of the problems confronting it. Communications between conveners, and between conveners and management, were sometimes at fault. For example, the absence of individual conveners at Conveners' Committee meetings sometimes held up proceedings, was due to their not being informed of the meeting, or remained simply unexplained. The inspectors' 'downer' which had been attended by the Group Director was itself very probably brought on by a breakdown in communications between the conveners and the Personnel Department. Complaints were raised at Combine Committee meetings of faulty communication between the Convener's Committees. Departmental stewards, particularly those representing day-workers, were quite often not informed of general shop stewards' meetings. General and departmental 'report-back' meetings came to be jettisoned without question, and some 'items for attention' lapsed into obscurity. Matters of more importance— for example, a decision by the J.S.S.C. to pursue a demand for increased rates of waiting-time payment—showed unusually slow progress in being put into procedure. Finally, some conveners started speaking privately and in deprecatory terms of their colleagues (though this might have indicated less a weakening of the conveners' 'morale' than the development of more personal rapport with the observer.)

The more general effects of this weakening of the shop steward organisation at the factory seemed to be an increasing scope for the activity of the more militant stewards and the apathy of others. The more militant stewards could the more easily pursue independent lines of action: the 'one out, all out' policy was a demonstration of this process. On the other hand, the less active stewards could more easily retain their posture. For example, when full-time officials wished to report back personally to the factory's stewards on the results of a meeting with management (which included discussion of matters of moment such as the claim for increased waiting-time rates, and the firm's alleged 'casual labour' policy), a meeting was arranged away from the factory and outside of working hours. It was postponed, as only nineteen stewards altogether attended. Only 35 stewards attended at the second attempt to hold this meeting—i.e., less than half of the factory's stewards—despite a careful choice of time and venue, and letters addressed individually to each steward from his official. In short, the authority of the factory's labour organisation was being eroded away, and it was unable to cope with the increased pressures being placed upon it at the time.

The weakening of the factory's labour organisation illustrated a more general point: the vulnerability of shop stewards to attack from both management and their own electorates. The conveners, in particular, were vulnerable both because of the relative inexperience of their new chairman and new member, and because they were administratively ill-equipped. Their organisation was being attacked by management at the same time as it was required to bear an increased load. Failures were reflected in a loss of control by the leadership. Under these circumstances, the conveners were driven to reluctant displays of militancy. The mass meetings of day-workers discussed in Section G could be seen as an early manifestation of a process which became emphatic during the waiting-time dispute. The conveners acquiesed in a mass strike because they were both ill-informed of existing agreements and unable to control their own organisation. What they needed from the management was constructive assistance.

J   A Conference on Industrial Relations

This conference took place after the events related in the previous sections, and like other top-level meetings between trade unionists and management which took place during the period of the study, it did not constitute a stage in the formal disputes procedure. It was a 'one-off': a special meeting between full-time officials of the trade unions and the conveners on the one hand, two of the firm's directors and its labour relations staff on the other. The chairman was the director of the employers' association. The meeting had the constitution of a Works Conference without the content—i.e., a dispute to be settled. The terms of reference were 'the state of industrial relations at the firm's local factories'. The conference is an appropriate subject for the final case study of this paper because it seemed to mark a climax in the industrial discontents of the factory during the period of the study. After the conference (though hardly as a result of it) the level of production rose and workshop discontent seemed to decline.

The conference was an implicit admission by the conveners that they felt that they could no longer cope with the situation at the factory: by handing it to their officials they were able to demonstrate to the departmental stewards and their members that action of some kind was being taken to meet the discontents.[1] For the position of the conveners had become very difficult: an average of about 1,500 men had been laid off work at short notice on each of nineteen days over a period of twenty-two weeks. As mentioned in the previous section, the conveners were losing control over the factory labour organisation, and shopfloor pressures were being expressed in many uncoordinated and almost unmanageable outbursts at departmental levels. While they had no interest in conducting guerilla warfare with the management, the conveners were being attacked by the latter on account of the intensification of overtime bans and sporadic 'downers' which contributed to further short-time working, and thus further discontent. Yet they could formulate no suitably general issue which could be taken through the official disputes procedure.

-----

(1)   Three weeks before the conference was held, after being informed of further short-time working to come and being unable to alter management's decision, the conveners reacted by stating that they were 'sick and tired of being messenger boys to the track stewards'. They invited the Industrial Relations Officer to call a stewards' meeting and come and address it himself. The J.S.S.C. Chairman conducted the meeting, thus indicating flexibility on the question of management attendance at stewards' meetings. (See section F, p. 53).

Three days before the conference, the problems had been presented to a gathering of full-time officials (and, again, less than a third of the factory's stewards had attended the meeting). The conveners had outlined what they saw as their main difficulties: that assembly workers were being treated by management as 'casual labour'; that threats to lay-off trackmen were being used by management to 'blackmail' other departments to work overtime; (1) that the extensive short-time working had not been organised so that workers could make the most rational use of their entitlements to unemployment benefits (the firm attributed the need for short-time working to labour disputes, did not therefore have to publicly acknowledge regular short-time working, and thus escaped adverse press publicity at the expense of its workers, the conveners said); and that the conveners could make no progress with the management on these matters. The officials adjourned to consider the matters raised, then re-convened—having agreed to approach the firm for a meeting with senior management as a matter of urgency. The urgency was reflected in the organisation of the conference to take place at such short notice.

The conference was held during a working day at the offices of the employers' association. The chairman first invited the trade union side to begin the discussion, and the six officials (one from each of the recognised unions) spoke for a short while in turn. The first to speak was the chairman of the District Committee of the C.S.E.U., and two of the later speakers were left to say only that they had nothing to add to what had already been said. There was, of course, considerable repetition, but the main points may be briefly paraphrased (from notes taken at the time): the stewards had complained of their members hardly having had a full week's work during the previous five months, and that this had also been a long period of unorganised short-time working. 'Unorganised' was stressed as having led to difficulties in obtaining unemployment benefits. The officials thought that the reason for the short-time working might have been an intention by the firm to lower and keep down the level of production of cars. The firm did not want to tell the world that their cars were not selling as they ought to have been. There was a belief that the firm did not want to produce the cars, and an explanation was required of the current trade position.

The shop stewards—the officials continued—had raised questions with management and had not received answers which satisfied them. Workers were being blamed for the factory's troubles, and were being sent home for what often seemed to be unnecessary reasons (specified by the Union spokesman of the moment only as 'this and that'). The stewards were doing their best to contain the workers, were perhaps losing control of their members, and were being castigated by the management to cover a shortage of orders. One official added that if the firm was making losses, then the trade unions did not want to damage it with publicity about the situation. After these opening salvoes the chairman offered an adjournment, but neither side thought it necessary.

---

(1) Overtime and short-time working which occurred together was felt to be inequitable by many workers, and raised tensions within the factory.

The management contingent consisted of the Works and Production Managers, the Personnel Executive, the Industrial Relations Officer, and the paintshop Superintendent. The Works Manager spoke first, expressing surprise that the Combine Committee members were not present.(1) He admitted the extensive short-time working, but suggested that the stewards had not informed the officials of all the reasons for it, such as strikes and overtime bans. He laid stress on these labour problems as having been a cause of lay-offs, and that they had made organised short-time working impossible. He added that the management did not lay men off work without consultation—one result of which had been management's agreement to the stewards', request to link Monday and Friday lay-offs each fortnight to facilitate claims for unemployment pay. This 'shouldn't be done by law' he claimed, but the firm did it because they had been asked to by the stewards. This preliminary sparring was cut short by a blunt question from an official: was the firm short of orders or not?

The Production Manager replied. He explained that about six months previously the firm had started to receive too many complaints from customers, and that rapid action had had to be taken. Distributors in the main export outlet had notified the firm that the then current paint process and finish was no longer acceptable to the market. The firm was to send no more of the cars painted in that way. While management had, at the time, been experimenting with a new paint process and paint facilities, they were now obliged to use these for production purposes. There was an attempt to squeeze fifteen months of experimentation into three months. The result had been a steady accumulation of cars on the sportsfield, until it had been decided that no more would be produced to be put outside to deteriorate. In short, there was no lack of orders, but the firm would not let cars out of the factory unless their condition was considered to be satisfactory. However, the firm seemed to be 'out of the wood now': although there was still a pool of unfinished cars, these were all of recent manufacture and could be cleared by the final line provided the latter kept working, i.e. had no overtime bans, go slows, or outright strikes.

The officials then asked about prospects—the 'forward programme', as they put it. The reply was that the firm wanted as many cars as could be produced as quickly as possible, provided they were of the required quality. Details were requested on actual numbers planned for: the hedging 'ifs and buts'—about both technical and labour problems—in the reply led to some heated exchanges between officials and management. It was suggested that other firms had had similar difficulties with the paint processes, but that they had not needed six months to deal with them. (This implied an accusation of mismanagement, but the argument was not conducted in these terms. Another line was followed instead.) There was a strong suspicion that if the cars had been wanted, the technical troubles

---

(1) It seemed that there had been a failure in communication between the Conveners' Committees—those at the other factories had not been told of the arrangements for the meeting. However, one of the officials replied to the point later in the discussion to the effect that the main problems were at the assembly factory anyway.

would soon have been overcome. Without proper forward planning, the official added, when one technical problem was overcome another could easily be contrived. He was not moved by an offer to refer to a management diary giving details of the technical problems, nor did any of the other officials respond to the invitation then made by the Production Manager to visit the factory and see the paint problems for themselves at any time. Management repeated that the problems had arisen because some of the plant was not designed to suit the paint material being used, and that there had been frequent failures in the material itself. The changes had themselves been forced on the firm by complaints. The arguments were becoming repetitive, and further discussion along these lines seemed unlikely to be productive. At this stage, the meeting tended to lose direction or purpose.

An attempt then followed to clarify the extent to which the short-time working had resulted from labour action as against the technical problems. Discussion was heated, as both sides tried, inconclusively, to shift blame onto the other. Particular events were not referred to: it was clear not only that the officials had been inadequately briefed, but that they were not likely to have sufficient detailed knowledge of the cases to be able to argue convincingly. The conveners might well have interjected at this stage had an opportunity arisen which would not have reflected adversely on their officials' grasp of the facts. The officials soon retreated from 'the chapter and verse on facts which should be kept at domestic level' to the more general 'state of industrial relations' existing at the factory. Their concern was said to cover the previous 18 months' period, but the terms of reference seemed too indefinite to be capable of fruitful exploration in the atmosphere which existed at the time, or without adequate preparation.

Discussion thus returned to the level of quibbling. For example, the Works Manager attacked the workers for being ungrateful to the firm in spite of all the waiting-time payments made when men were standing about. The firm had at great expense decided to put cars on the sportsfield, men were kept at work in good faith, and they did not appreciate it— he said. Officials referred to his earlier statement about unemployment benefits and the law, rejecting the implication that there was anything underhand in organising short-time working so as to be able to maximise benefits. Exployment Exchange officials were said to be generally very helpful in this regard. The meeting had now lasted for only just over an hour, but the Production Director and one of the officials had already excused themselves and left for other appointments, and the chairman attempted to draw proceedings to a rapid close.

The final ten minutes of the meeting were used by the conveners—now vocal for the first time—to pursue what for them was of most importance: work prospects for the weeks immediately ahead. They needed to be able to convince a generally discontented or even hostile J.S.S.C. that progress had been made. The firm was now 'out of the wood'—but would there be 'full production'? The Industrial Relations Officer replied that the factory was adequately manned for 'full production', then asked in what form the men would prefer any further short-time to be taken. But—he hastened to try to reassure them—workers could be told that they could be working full-time provided the bodyshop would rescind an over-time ban imposed that very morning, and which management had only just heard about, and 'excepting unforeseen circumstances'. A rider was added that some supply departments had built up large stocks, and might well be put on short time during the following weeks.

This was scarcely reassuring. The paint shop Superintendent and the chairman of the J.S.S.C. (a paint shop specialist) agreed, however, that the technical problems which had been holding up production seemed to have been solved. One convener then said that their confidence would be based on results over the following three weeks, at which the Works Manager interjected that 'results' would not be due to 'this conference', and that the position had been steadily improving for some weeks already. There seemed to be little more to be said, and the chairman then closed the conference. As the officials dispersed, the conveners exchanged the opinion that—as far as they were concerned—the meeting had served little purpose other than the registering of a protest.

It was difficult to avoid the conclusion that the conveners were largely right in this judgement. The Group Director might have been expected to attend a meeting of this kind, yet his absence caused no comment. There had been no clear issue over which the meeting could get to grips—the operation of domestic procedures had not been capable of distilling such an issue. An outstanding managerial responsibility to inform and consult with the conveners or trade unions in advance about the expected dislocations which technical alterations would create was not mentioned at the conference. Nor had any serious factual analyses been presented by either side—e.g., of the incidence and causes of stoppages or lay-offs.

What had been most immediately noticeable about the conference was the imperturbability with which management had handled the charges which were made, and the absence of any attempt on the part of the trade union officials to ensure that short-time working would be handled any differently in the future. On the matter of the charges themselves the officials had agreed—during the half-hour briefing session with the conveners before the meeting (and at which only three officials had been present)—that the main question they would pursue was the state of the firm's order book. This they saw as the crucial consideration in attempts to make progress on an acceptable policy of short-time scheduling. Management had admitted a loss of orders, but had turned the argument to technical considerations and the intransigence of some groups of workers. Discussion on future policy had been largely forestalled by statements that the technical difficulties had already been overcome. The terms of reference of the conference had been more grandiose or diffuse than was either necessary or practical.

The officials were not equipped to handle detailed discussion about particular events that had taken place in the factory. When they had attempted to do so, they had soon seen the need to retreat to consideration of wider issues, or be made to look foolish. On other occasions, perhaps, the conveners may have come to their assistance, but in this instance the situation had not lent itself to intervention by the conveners. The officials had given them no lead-in; the detailed charges raised had already been flatly rejected by the management; and the conveners, as already

discussed, had been in a state of some demoralisation. They had already
made explicitly clear to the officials (and the observer) their general
belief that if issues could not be solved inside the factory, it was unlikely
that they would be solved outside it. However, the points made here
about the role of full-time officials should not be taken to imply general
criticism. Their schedule of duties leaves little time for detailed briefing, and in this instance, the conference had been arranged at very short
notice indeed. The general nature of the terms of reference did not help
them: there had been little scope for bringing their wide experience to
bear on particular problems.

The conference did, however, serve to illustrate an interesting attitude
to the firm on the part of the trade union side. This appeared in the official's remark that publicity about difficulties the firm might be experien-
cing could damage both management and labour. It was a view which had
been expressed on other occasions by conveners and departmental stewards. It was most succintly put during the course of a Combine Committee meeting, when it was said that 'the problem is that if the firm
don't want the cars, it is bad enough. If they announce this, it is even
worse'. The problem was 'bad enough' because production schedules
were a managerial prerogative: no pressure or protest from stewards or
unions was believed to be capable of forcing the firm to make cars if it
did not choose to do so. Unfavourable publicity would be 'even worse' in
that it was thought that it would damage the esteem of the firm's products, the firm's market position, and wages and condition of its workers.
In short, stewards and trade union officials concurred with what they believed to be a longstanding policy of the firm: to avoid public mention of
short-time working. Nor was this merely a verbal concurrence: at
J.S.S.C. meetings, the suggestion had been made more than once to 'have
a mass meeting in the centre of the city on the next day off to protest at
lay-offs and with the press invited to be present'. These suggestions had
been side-stepped by the conveners.

PART III

K   Some Conclusions

It seems sensible to start with a statement of aims and limitations. The purpose of this concluding section is to draw together more closely some of the major impressions standing out from the welter of information about industrial relations at the factory which the method of study inevitably presented, and to consider causes or explanations rather than to propose explicit remedies. The strikes are placed first in a ranking of the impressions. The structural machinery of industrial relations, and the functioning of procedures, are then discussed. Some of the limitations of this study were mentioned in the introductory section: this concluding section has limitations of a different kind. While many of the points made would be valid for most of the larger British car assembly factories, generalisation of this kind is not attempted here. Then again, industrial relations at the factory can scarcely be comprehensively considered without reference to the national and more-narrowly industrial systems of institutions within which they occur. It is clear from the preceding sections, for example, that fluctuations in consumer demand for cars have imposed a heritage of insecurity amongst workers about employment and earnings, while many features of the factory's wage structure are derived from and maintained by the firm's adherence to the engineering wage system. This paper does no more than acknowledge the presence of these 'external' influences. So much by way of prolegomena.

Strikes are the most spectacular and frequently used measures of industrial discontents. Yet is was not possible to determine how many strikes had taken place during the period spent by the researcher at the factory. No consolidated record had been maintained of even the more major events in which strikers left the factory premises, let alone of the 'downers' which had been brief, departmental affairs. Conveners had neither time for nor concern with keeping records of this kind, while the Personnel Executive held that he and his department had been too busy to do so. If a stringent definition of strikes is adopted—one which would include events like a fifteen-minute march of protest around an office block during working hours, and workers' meetings which substantially over-ran the dinner-break—there had been a minimum of thirty strikes. This figure is probably an underestimate of the actual number: it was derived from questioning and the limited records kept by some departments. But no estimate is possible of the overall proportions of various issues in dispute, the numbers of strikers involved, or the times the stoppages had lasted. Most of them took place on a departmental scale and were short—lasting no more than an hour or two. They were sufficiently frequent to be regarded as a normal part of working life. Experience would suggest that—unless large-scale lay-offs and reduced bonus-earnings seemed likely to result—they were of little interest to workers outside the departments in which they occured (even when taking place in full view of workers in contiguous departments).

The frequency of strikes at the factory raises questions about their 'status' or classification, the representativeness of the sample chosen for presentation as case studies in this paper, and their effects on production. To take 'status' first, the firm found it unnecessary to distinguish between 'unconstitutional' strikes (i.e. those which took place before the exhaustion of all stages in the engineering disputes procedure) and 'unofficial' strikes (i.e. those not having publicly-acknowledged union approval). All of the strikes fell into both categories—suggesting a limited usefulness in practice of this basis of classification. Secondly, while it was not possible to analyse the issues in dispute in all of the stoppages during the period it has been possible to compare the issues in publicly-reported strikes in the factory over a number of years with those in the other car firms. The factory's record is not untypical, and the general distribution of issues has been used to guide the choice of strikes to present as case studies. The bonus scheme and 'waiting-time' disputes arose out of the wage-structure, and the 'breach of procedure' affair was an amalgam of management, employment, and 'trade-union' issues—all occurring in a matrix of discontent over short-time working and fluctuating earnings. The economic costs of strikes are scarcely calculable and are generally over-emphasised. Here it can only be suggested that, with a drop in demand for the models assembled at the factory, with an accumulation of cars about the premises, and with time required to improve a new paint process, management might well have welcomed the respite granted by at least some of the strikes. An impression gained by the observer was that, in any event, production facilities were rather flexible, and that even quite large strikes might have no observable effect on the achievement of weekly production targets.

Moving now to the subject of causation, it may be more convenient to start by rejecting a number of explanations sometimes put forward to account for the high strike-liability of car workers, and which were inappropriate to this factory. The first of these explanations suggests that the strikes are in large measure due to the inherent nature of assembly-line work, or the technology of the industry. The evidence—in the form of a considerable literature[1]— is based on the attitudes of assembly-line workers to their jobs. But in this factory, men did not complain or speak spontaneously about the characteristics of assembly-line work—of the 'tensions of the tracks'. Trackmen were envied by very many dayworkers, and their comparatively high earnings were not held to be due to greater skill requirements or more difficult working conditions. There were not

---

(1)   This literature is reviewed in 'Strikes and dissatisfaction with assembly-line work in car factories', Cambridge Opinion, 45, November, 1966. (D.A.E. Reprint No. 262.)

infrequent requests made at the Personnel Department by dayworkers for transfer to assembly work, in spite of the knowledge that it was not the policy of the firm to make such transfers. The most common complaint of trackmen themselves arose over involuntary periods spent waiting for work, and over lay-offs. They wanted to keep working—not to take breaks from the 'pressures' of their jobs. Other evidence refuting the applicability of the explanation is even more convincing: it was apparent that the issues in disputes seldom arose from the inherent nature of the work itself, and it was clear that many of the strikes were undertaken by departments or groups of workers who were not 'track-paced'.

Another cluster of explanations for the strike-liability of car factories relies on attributes of the car workers themselves rather than of their work. The arguments take a number of different forms. Car workers are variously held to be ageing (and hence becoming more irritable and predisposed to taking strike action), inexperienced or 'green' (and hence unfamiliar with work in car factories and the facilities available for the peaceable settlement of disputes), and provoked by a few 'agitators' into actions which are not justifiable by reference to 'objective' wages or working conditions (being thus easily and persistently led by the nose). But two out of five of the workers at the factory were under the age of thirty five, three out of four were under the age of fifty, and there was no observable tendency for militancy and greying hair to occur together. The ageing argument is an implausible one, anyway. Nor were the workers unaware of 'procedure' (obscure in detail as it was): it was referred to quite frequently on the shop floor, management admitted delays in its operation, and workers interpreted their experience as justifying an attitude of 'do nothing and you get nothing'. Finally, the 'agitator' theory was not seriously suggested to the observer by any manager or worker at the factory—and was often refuted during discussions. While one of the conveners remarked that difficulties sometimes arose because of the 'personalities' of particular stewards, there was no suggestion of an 'ideological' (1) implication in these cases, and the difficulties were not suggested to persist in the absence of grounds for unrest in the departments concerned. Another convener suggested that 'dull stewards cause more trouble than cunning ones'.

The strikes could not be attributed to the activities of a tightly-controlled or militant shop steward organisation—either at the factory or drawing support or inspiration from steward or trade union organisations ex-

----

(1) The absence of communist or 'Trot' influence at the factory has already been mentioned. It is interesting that when a Christmas appeal on behalf of 'troublemakers' who had been sacked from Ford was received and considered by the J.S.S.C., a proposal that the letter be merely 'noted' was passed with only three votes cast against it. Communism was not directly referred to although one avowed anti-communist seemed to choose his words carefully. The weightiest reason for rejecting the appeal seemed to be that 'there are 45,000 members at Ford who can deal with it'.

ternal to the factory. Departmental stewards sometimes recommended strike action; they also sometimes did their best to prevent their members from taking such action. They were generally concerned about the 'constitutionality' of their conduct, and, on balance, seemed more concerned to prevent strikes occurring, to limit such actions where they could not prevent them, and to induce strikers to return to work. This attitude could be attributed to a number of factors: for example, to the practical and sometimes tactical need to assess the priorities amongst a number of current issues, to the fact that stewards were subject to managerial sanctions of various kinds, to an awareness of the loss of earnings by strikers and others laid-off in consequence, and sometimes, to what might be described as a seeming preference for a quiet life. Many stewards—when asked—said that they had taken on the job unwillingly, and often only because there had been nobody else in the department who would accept the task. In these cases, the job itself would present a challenge to some, while others would retain there attitudes of reluctance and would hesitate to raise issues with supervision unless hard pressed by their members to do so. Poor attendance at stewards' meetings which were held away from the factory (and even sometimes at those held at the factory) was one indication of the extent of this posture.

In the case of the conveners, the position was more clear-cut. While they might individually induce or support a demonstration by their own members, such activity was almost incidental to their avowed and collective policy of keeping as many men at work as possible (for at least a normal working week). This policy was not pious but was put into practice (although with varying degrees of success). Conveners generally had more than enough problems on their hands to discourage any interest in provoking more, and the working days of those who were full-time negotiators were observed to be exacting and often arduous. They once spoke of themselves as a 'fire brigade', and—at least during the period of study— 'compulsive comparison' between factories or between departments was an inappropriate and almost inarticulate guide to policy on wage and other issues. While the conveners—and some departmental stewards—had more or less regular contact with stewards in other factories in the locality (at the gatherings held at their trade union offices), observation of this kind of meeting between shop stewards in the car industry more generally suggests that there is little exchange of information about factory wage rates or earnings which is systematic or detailed enough to be of assistance in actual negotiations—over piece-work prices or work-loads, for instance. In short, the conveners and shop steward organisation at the factory did not appear as a driving force behind the labour unrest, but could more validly be regarded as 'shock absorbers' of the industrial relations machinery. The suggestion that trade unions should prevent unofficial action by their members by 'disciplining' their shop stewards in some way would be inappropriate to situations of this kind.

Although the strikes were all undertaken without official trade union approval, they could not be regarded either as having been directed 'against' the unions or as constituting expressions of specific dissatisfaction with the full-time officials. On the other hand, the officials were certainly not inducing the strikes—although one of them said that he might occasionally indicate that a demonstration by his members could be helpful at a point in negotiations with managements (and the metal fitters' official's involvement at one point during the 'breach of procedure' affair seemed to be of this kind). It was noticeable that workers at the factory very rarely spoke of their full-time officials—either generally or in more personal terms. A group of younger trackmen did express the opinion that their union and its officials were of little value to them, but this was at a time when a 'card check' was being conducted (to reduce arrears in the payment of contributions); it showed a lack of appreciation of the role of unions and the work-load of officials, and was contested by older workers who were present. The average worker—and not a few stewards—very seldom saw his union officials at the workplace (or elsewhere, for that matter), and it is understandable that the relevance of officials to workplace situations seemed to have been only tenuously perceived.

The relations between conveners and union officials were, once again of a different—and more complicated—kind. Firstly, conveners would—almost of necessity—have close working relationships with the officials of their own trade unions. It was their duty to report formally and periodically to their officials about rates and general conditions at the factory, and in their interests to keep the officials informed of disputes which showed signs that they might develop into situations requiring the officials' assistance or involve members of other unions. Secondly, if a convener (or management, as in the case of the 'breach of procedure' strike) brought an official into the practical conduct of a dispute—as against merely seeking his advice and keeping him informed—the other conveners said that this action could inhibit conciliation by the Conveners' Committee itself, even at the earliest stages in a dispute and before members of other unions might become directly affected by it. For the Conveners' Committee would have to take care to avoid compromising the actions of the official, and any exchange of advice between the committee and an official would of necessity be a delicate operation. Clashes of policy might not be uncommon under these circumstances—if only because support for militant action by one union would almost inevitably produce short-time working and reduced earnings for members of other unions. That these considerations did not inhibit the everyday functioning of the Conveners' Committee was due, partly to the infrequency with which officials were directly involved in disputes, and partly to the strong bonds of common interest between the conveners. The S.M.W.U. convener's statement that the 'town policy' of his union—protecting its autonomy of action—was not an inflexible one (reported in section F), was one indication of the strength of these bonds.

Thirdly, there were occasions when the shop stewards' organisation would decide to 'bring in the officials' collectively. Neither the J.S.S.C. nor the Conveners' Committee were quick to adopt or suggest this course of action. For example, officials were not asked to attend the mass meetings of day-workers who were on strike over the bonus system—even though the first of these meetings had been arranged during the previous week, and the second might well have involved a continuation of the strike (as had the first). And it was only in the final stages of negotiation about the 'provocative and ill-timed' notice that the J.S.S.C. decided to ask the officials for their assistance. The arrangement of the 'conference on industrial relations' followed a collective approach by the shop stewards to the officals only after months of shop-floor discontent, and some demoralisation of the labour organisation at the factory. The reluctance to make fuller use of trade union officials was consistent with the beliefs expressed by conveners (and the management) that issues were better settled within the factory than outside of it.

The interrelations between union members, their shop stewards, and trade union officials, are cental to the contention that the multiplicity of unions in some factories is a major cause of strikes. One aspect of this contention—i.e., that a mixed union membership combined with a geographical or area system of workshop representation allows shop stewards considerable autonomy of action vis-a-vis their unions—has already been implicitly rejected as an explanation of the strikes at the factory, at least to the extent that the shop stewards were not actively fomenting unrest. Other aspects of the contention are that inter-union rivalry for members and for work are issues in disputes, and that there are difficulties over differing union rules and policies which impede the development of expeditious approaches to common problems. As already mentioned (in section D), there seemed to be little concern at the factory amongst the workers about the particular trade union to which a man might belong. It seemed to be neither a topic of conversation nor a question asked of fellow-workers—membership of one of the appropriate unions being taken for granted. In those cases where a shop or occupation was closed to members of one union the question did not arise either: agreement and understanding had long been reached about spheres of interest.

Amongst the shop stewards there were occasional frictions and tensions between those representing different unions (as there were between representatives of the same union). In at least some of these few cases, 'personality' differences were as likely an explanation as membership of different unions. The reservations expressed by two of the conveners about the policies and intentions of unions other than their own, and about the characters of some of their fellow conveners, had gossip and general talk about the 'poaching' of members as their main constituents: their possible effect on industrial relations was difficult to assess but could not have been more than slight. Then again, the relations between the full-time officials is a subject about which this study can offer little information. When together at meetings, the officials' relations appeared cordial but slightly restrained. Some of the most pointed remarks about other unions were made by officials at branch or stewards' meetings within their own organisations, or in private discussion, and were mostly about the alleged poaching intentions or activities of the rival organisations. Officials were certainly concerned lest information given to the researcher—about membership and the distribution of shop stewards, for example—should find its way to the other union offices.

To sum up this consideration of the contention that multiple unionism might be held to account for strikes in this car factory, it was clear that the reasons given by strikers and those most concerned in disputes at the time for their actions were not about inter-union relations. The manifestations of union rivalry seemed to increase with increasing distance from the shop floor, ascending the shop steward hierarchy, into the district offices of the trade unions. This feature in consistent with what might be expected on grounds of plausibility. But multi-unionism—if not an issue in strikes of its own right—could certainly be held to have a kind of negative effect. The presence of different unions in the factory could be a complicating factor which might delay the settlement of some disputes (as in the 'breach of procedure' affair): the possibility of a conflict between the policies of the J.S.S.C. and those of individual unions is inherent in the situation. For all these reasons, it would be difficult to suggest that—apart from its questionable appropriateness on other grounds—an effective supervision of the J.S.S.C. or Conveners' Committee could be exercised by a committee of full time officials functioning under the existing trade union organisational arrangements.

The factors which, on the other hand, do seem to be most relevant to an explanation of the strike-proneness of the factory, will be discussed under three broad headings: the issues in disputes, the procedures for settling these issues, and the management and labour organisations. While no analysis is possible of the issues involved in all of the strikes it is clear that the larger events (and very probably the majority of all the strikes as well) were mostly about matters which could be regarded as self-explanatory. With the major exception of the 'breach of procedure' strike, what the workers said they were striking about could be taken very largely at face value: the situations did not seem to call for a consideration of subconscious aggression and hostility, or subversive agitation. In the strikes examined in detail, the main discontents were about the wage structure and payments system, the insecurity of job rights and earnings, or a concern for the protection of trade union functions. The factors which do not fit easily into this classification of issues are those about 'personality' in the breach of procedure affair, and those concerning 'misunderstandings'. The early stages of the 'breach of procedure' strike (i.e. both the concern for the control of labour recruitment, and the desire to demonstrate to men and management an undiminished strength of organisation despite a change of convener) fit without too much difficulty into the protection of trade unionism category. The muddle and misunderstandings did not seem to be merely or even mainly a result of poor 'communications', but seemed largely inherent in the conjunction of complicated social situations and inadequate institutions.

Seasonal and cyclical fluctuations in the general demand for cars, and in the fortunes of the firm's models, had fostered a heritage of insecurity amongst the car workers. There was long experience of employment and earnings' instability, and an expectation that this would continue. The instability seemed the main cause of the general, widely-dispersed discontent amongst the workers at the facotry. The discontent was expressed less in demands that there should not be such instability than that the hardships should be distributed more equitably between departments and with more concern on management's part for the well-being of workers. For example, overtime working by some departments whilst others were working only on three days in a week was regarded as unfair, and there was pressure for the transfer of men from one department to another wherever this might be practicable (though the 'practicality' was itself a source of some dispute between stewards and managers, and between stewards themselves—even where 'spheres of union interest' were not affected). Then again the months of disorganised or unscheduled short-time working, and the laying-off of trackmen at short notice, seemed as central to the 'casual labour' charges as the laying-off itself. Other car firms in the area were held to operate more responsibly in this regard: it was said that their workers would be told that, say, a four-day week would be in effect for a stated number of weeks ahead, and would not be left to wonder about work prospects—often from day to day. There was also the wide-spread belief, held by some managers as well, that small disputes—for which the trade union side could publicly be blamed—were being used as one way of regulating production.

Wages at the factory were a source of dissatisfaction amongst the workers in two main respects. The first lay in the somewhat arbitrary and variable relation between individual or departmental effort and earnings, as demonstrated, for example, in the case of the bonus disputes in the spare parts department. The second lay in the size of the earnings' differentials between trackmen and day-workers. Day-workers felt that the skills and effort required by assembly work did not warrant the differences in pay between the two groups. Trackmen would normally earn more than half as much again as day-workers, and—while day-workers acknowledged that they were less subject to lay-offs than trackmen—at least some of them took this to be recognition by the firm that they earned too little to be able to absorb lay-offs (at least one departmental manager had expressed the same view). The day-workers resented also having to work some regular overtime for what they regarded as a living wage (in contrast to most trackmen, who worked only a limited amount of overtime during three or four months in the year).

The wage system and structure at the factory could be held to be sources of dissatisfaction in other ways. For example, the bonus schemes were complicated and easily misunderstood. They also 'penalised' groups according to the amount of overtime worked in their departments. An individual who worked many hours of overtime would thus be held to have gained his high earnings at the expense of the other workers—which led to resentment at any uneven allocation of overtime working between individuals. This resentment was in addition to that arising from an alleged use by supervision of offers of overtime work as a kind of reward for general co-operativeness and for a willingness to accept overtime at short notice. Another source of dissatisfaction lay, of course, in the system of rate-fixing for jobs which were, because of the nature of the industry, subject to fairly frequent changes. Each new bargain over a piece-work price could well introduce a 'distortion' into the earnings structure which would at some time require 'corrective' action by other groups of workers. But 'compulsive comparisons' of this kind within the factory seemed to have been muted during the period of the study, although the pressures arising in this manner could partially account for statements that groups of workers acted selfishly in setting out to increase their own earnings irrespective of the effects of their actions on other groups. As one of the firm's managers put it: 'We cultivate a battleground, and then blame the workers for fighting on it'.

Trade union issues—broadly defined—were not as important in the genesis of strikes as either the instability of employment and earnings or
the wage structure and wage system. Trade union relations—arising out
of multiple unionism at the factory—have already been discussed: their
contribution to the factory's strike-proneness was marginal. Nor were
the trade unions or conveners in any sense fighting for recognition by
the management. On the contrary, in formally recognising and consulting
the local Combine Committee—and in granting it facilities—the firm's
senior management had adopted a policy in advance of many other
managements in the area at the time. Management collected the contributions from workers to a Shop Stewards' Fund, accepted a 'union shop',
and had agreed to assist the unions in 'disciplining' workers who fell
seriously behind in their union contributions by withholding employment
until the arrears had been paid. In practice, however, management attitudes to the factory's labour organisation were ambivalent and erratic
(as will be discussed below). Those trade union issues which were
matters of dispute seemed to involve either a protection by the stewards
of their status and organisation (as in their reaction to the 'provocative
and ill-timed' notice in the breach of procedure strike), or more limited
departmental skirmishes about matters such as the appropriate number
of shop stewards or the adequacy of consultation. Disputes about trade
unionism were over the interpretation, extension, or protection of rights,
and not about the principle of recognition itself.

Management's ambivalent approach to labour organisation at the factory
had been noted by informed observers outside the factory. It was clearly
reflected in the differences between the policy and the practice of industrial relations, and was present at all levels of the management hierarchy.
In comparison with the policy of recognition, the management machinery
for the conduct of industrial relations was undeveloped—almost primitive
—in relation to the size of the factory and its long history of labour unrest. There was (at the time of the study) no industrial relations specialist at senior management level, and, although the Works Manager
had been formally responsible for the function, he shared this function
to some extent with the Production Manager. When trade union officials
could make no progress in negotiations with these managers, they
approached the Group Director—who had himself occasionally, and
seemingly at random, intervened in industrial relations matters at
departmental level. The Personnel Executive seemed to have had a
lower status than the other executives (and was said to have been paid
a salary lower than his title would suggest). The 'personnel' function
was limited in scope. For example, there was no training of operatives,
stewards, or supervision—either in industrial skills or industrial relations. Accident records were of the statutory minimum. There were
no factory-based figures on absenteeism, lateness, or strikes. The first
labour turnover analysis had been produced only three months before
this study began. It seemed as though the granting of facilities to the
factory's labour organisation had been regarded by management as sufficient in itself to have prevented labour unrest, or that the facilities
obscured a managerial unwillingness to come to terms with trade
unionism.

On the other hand, the shop steward organisation had also seemed ill-equipped to meet the pressures which had been placed upon it. These pressures had come primarily from the shop floor in the form of demands from discontented workers for high and stabilised employment and earnings—a demand which the conveners had believed to be difficult or impossible to achieve under the circumstances at the time. Attempts to control the manifestations of these discontents had had only limited success: the conveners had steadily lost their authority over the factory's labour organisation as the pressures had mounted. It seemed that management had misunderstood the function which the conveners had been trying to fulfil, for, while generally attempting to keep men at work, they had been accused of being 'troublemakers' by the Group Director, and the facilities granted to shop stewards were being reduced. For example, management complained that too many shop steward meetings were being held during working hours, an attempt seems to have been made to restrict the conveners' use of factory telephones, while their movement about the works was inhibited by requests that periodically they report their whereabouts to the Personnel Department. They were asked to spend more time at the bench.(1) It is very likely that a Conveners' Committee, administratively more efficient and carrying more authority, would have interceded at an early stage in the breach of procedure strike, prevented the 'one out, all out' motion from being carried, and could have maintained a file of agreements which would have been referred to at the beginning of the 'waiting time' dispute (although one could also speculate about the uses to which a strong—e.g. well organised and well-informed—labour organisation might be put when production requirements were more pressing, or technical problems less troublesome than they seemed to have been at the time of the study).

The shop steward organisation was fulfilling, if in a clumsy and inefficient way, a number of useful 'managerial' functions. It aimed, ultimately, to keep men at work and to control—even discipline—union members. The senior shop stewards were involved in the enforcement of collective agreements, and concerned with the implementation (even planning) and co-ordination of many everyday details of production—such as the trans-

---

(1) Management had avoided an open clash over these restrictions of some of the facilities granted to shop stewards because they had not been granted formally in the first place. For example, the fiction of work 'at the bench' by the full-time conveners had been maintained, while stewards' movement passes had fallen into general disuse—but could have been revived by request had management chosen this course. An example of the genesis of uncertain or informal stewards' 'rights' occurred during the period of study. When approached, management had recognised that some departmental stewards required to spend more time than others on 'union business' at the factory, and that this had caused problems in the payment of such stewards. It had been indicated that management would connive at the informal allocation to these stewards of particular jobs known to be less arduous than others, thus allowing them to 'make time' more easily by working ahead or by catching up with schedules after a break.

fers of men around the factory, the scheduling of overtime or short-time working, and the recruitment and training of labour. Their efficient performance of these functions was hampered to some extent by multi-unionism, which made a clear and consistent focus of leadership from outside the plant difficult to perceive. But more important hindrances were the lack of adequate administrative facilities, intermittent managerial obstructiveness about the facilities which had been obtained, and the absence of advance information and consultation about major problems—the difficulties and dislocation expected to result from the change-over of paint processes, for example. Nor was the obscurity and inconsistency of the disputes' procedure of general assistance to the factory's shop steward organisation in the performance of its managerial functions.

The rules or procedures for the avoidance or settlement of disputes by management and shop stewards were relevant to the pattern of industrial relations at the factory in several respects. Firstly, there were occasions when the 'correctness' of procedure was uncertain. For example, the appointment of the Industrial Relations Officer had introduced changes into the procedure about which there was some initial confusion. Departmental stewards could not always be assumed to be well-briefed in procedural matters, while formal and informal procedures were almost inextricably co-existent. Secondly, the functioning of procedure itself could become a matter of dispute, as in the breach of procedure affair. Thirdly, there had been a history of delays by management in taking matters through procedure. Then again, and apart from the speed with which procedure could function, there was the 'perishability' of some issues themselves, which necessarily required that a settlement be reached within a very short time—failing which matters would tend to arrange themselves to the detriment of the aggrieved party. Examples of such issues would be dismissals,(1) 'provocative' notices, compensation for the fitting of non-standard though usable components, and unsatisfactory working conditions such as fumes or insufficient heating. Enforcing the performance of an agreement—as in the bonus disputes in the spare parts department—was a similar perishable issue.

Many workers also felt that if satisfactory settlement of an issue could not be obtained at departmental level, there was a possibility that the issue might become distorted or merged with other issues at the higher levels of procedure. For example, the storemen in the spare parts department wanted to keep their bonus issue—and the protest actions— separate from those of other departments, while the breach of procedure affair provides a (perhaps extreme) example of the way in which issues

---

(1) During the period at the factory, a man in the spare parts department was summarily dismissed by the superintendent for absenteeism. He was reinstated within a matter of hours, following the staging of a 'downer' by the other storemen. Some of these storemen reported an earlier case in which one of the junior foremen had been summarily dismissed for his 'blind eye' to smoking by storemen in a prohibited area, and had also been reinstated after a brief demonstration by the storemen on his behalf.

may change during the course of a dispute. The fear of issues becoming 'lost' in the higher stages of procedure, together with the uncertainty about the constitution of procedure itself, the heritage of delays in its operation, and the need for very speedy handling of some issues, go some way towards explaining a common attitude amongst the car workers that 'if you do nothing, you get nothing'—of which the supervisory counterpart was that workers' demands have to be opposed on principle, 'or things would soon get out of hand'. In short, there was a need for adequate procedural machinery at workshop level—to at least clarify if not settle issues before they reached the 'official' stages outside the factory.

The heavy reliance on informal procedures at the factory has already been mentioned (in section E). The engineering 'Procedure—Manual Workers' agreement serves to encourage it, and the conveners, for their part, were generally in favour of informality. For example, when there was dispute over what had been said at an earlier meeting, management offered the Combine Committee the presence of a shorthand-typist at these joint meetings to record the proceedings verbatim. The chairman of the Combine Committee asked: 'would this engender a good spirit?' and the matter was dropped. Another of the conveners said that 'in general, anyway, if you ask for formal meetings you get only formal answers'—implying that most issues were satisfactorily settled without being referred to the higher stages of formal domestic procedure (a distinction between formal and informal procedures at the departmental levels being rather unreal). While, on balance, the informal procedures had seemed to offer an expeditious and speedy settlement of problems, they were subject to the same kind of disadvantage which has already been mentioned in connection with the informality of some of the shop stewards' facilities. Their functioning was subject to the goodwill of both parties, and they could be put into abeyance unilaterally to suit the changing convenience or strategy of either party. For example, management could sometimes refuse to negotiate under the duress of a strike, while, in the course of the breach of procedure dispute, a convener refused to accept the 'informal' presence of the Personnel Executive at a meeting held at the Industrial Relations Officer's stage of procedure. Informality avoids the establishment of clear 'rights'.(1)

Finally, a picture of the factory's industrial relations which presented management and workers in positions of entrenched embattlement would be misleading. Statements of mutual mistrust were only one partial manifestation of a wider complex of attitudes and beliefs which influenced decision-making in the day-to-day conduct of industrial relations. To be set off against such statements were those by management which acknowledged the role of the shop steward organisation in the solution of 'managerial' problems about production and people, and statements by workers and their stewards acknowledging that their welfare depended

---

(1) A convener at another car factory put the matter in different terms: 'the "hot line" works in your favour only when you're batting'— meaning that there were no agreed rules or criteria for ranking disputes in order of importance or need for 'priority' attention.

to a considerable extent on the prosperity of the firm. Public displays of contentious issues had been deliberately avoided by the conveners because they might have been harmful to the firm and its workers. Attempts to alter the pattern of the factory's industrial relations would clearly have to take account of these wider systems of attitudes and beliefs as well as the adequacy of the organisational structures and procedural machinery for handling differences of interest between management and the workers. But it would seem that the attempts would have to take most account of the nature of the issues which were arising as the subject-matter of the disputes themselves—of their background causes and of the implications for future policies.